Ext. New York City:
Discover The Reel New York On Location

About The Author

Dallas King is a self-confessed movie nerd who first began writing about film in 2009 when he watched and reviewed every movie on Empire Magazine's list of the 500 Greatest Films Of All-Time in 365 days.

Since then he has written articles for Clothes On Film, The Guardian Online and Empire Online. He has his own blogs at Championship Celluloid and Ext. New York City and contributes a weekly film column to his local newspaper.

Dallas currently lives in Aberdeen where he works at his local independent cinema, the Belmont Filmhouse, but as Woody Allen would say *"New York was his town, and it always would be."*

Ext. New York City is his first book.

Ext. New York City:
Discover The Reel New York On Location

Dallas King

Dallas King
2015

Copyright © 2015 All text by Dallas King. Images by Derek King & Dallas King

All rights reserved. This book or any portion thereof may not be reproduced or used in any manner whatsoever without the express written permission of the publisher except for the use of brief quotations in a book review or scholarly journal.

First Printing: 2015

ISBN 978-1326-39561-2

Championship Celluloid Ltd.
17 Mid Stocket Road
Aberdeen, AB15 5JL, UK

www.championshipcelluloid.blogspot.com

Dedication

To Lucy.

When you know you want to spend the rest of your life with someone,
you want the rest of your life to start as soon as possible.
You made that possible when you said yes at Sutton Place.
This is for you.

Contents

Acknowledgements xi

Foreword xiii

Introduction 1

Top Ten Films: The Naked City (1948) 3

Top Ten Locations: The Empire State Building 5

Apocalypse New... York 7

Top Ten Films: Sweet Smell Of Success (1957) 9

Top Ten Locations: Times Square 11

Broadway 13

Top Ten Films: Breakfast At Tiffany's (1961) 15

Top Ten Locations: The Statue Of Liberty 17

Martin Scorsese 20

Top Ten Films: Taxi Driver (1976) 22

Top Ten Locations: Grand Central Terminal 24

Woody Allen 26

Top Ten Films: Manhattan (1979) 28

Top Ten Locations: Central Park 30

Horror 32

Top Ten Films: Ghostbusters (1984) 34

Top Ten Locations: New York Public Library 36

Holidays	38
Top Ten Films: Wall Street (1985)	40
Top Ten Locations: Rockefeller Center	42
Sex In The City	45
Top Ten Films: When Harry Met Sally (1989)	47
Top Ten Locations: Washington Square Park	49
Spike Lee	51
Top Ten Films: Do The Right Thing (1989)	53
Top Ten Locations: Brooklyn Bridge	54
Superhero City	56
Top Ten Films: Spider-Man (2002)	59
Top Ten Locations: Coney Island	61
Gangs Of New York	63
Planes, Trains And Automobiles	64
Hotels	67
Restaurants	71
Bars	75
Shops	78
Museums	82
Cinemas	85
Maps: Upper West Side	88
Maps: Upper East Side	90
Maps: Theatre District	92
Maps: Midtown	94

Maps: Chelsea, Flatiron, Gramercy Park 96
Maps: West Village, Greenwich Village, East Village ... 98
Maps: Financial District, Downtown, Brooklyn 100
Map: Central Park 102
Location Index 105
Filmography 109

Acknowledgements

Lucy, my soulmate and Editor-In-Chief. Your endless love, support, encouragement and belief in my abilities as a writer are a constant inspiration to me to achieve my dreams. Thank you for all your advice and not being afraid to tell me the truth and get out your red pen!

Mum and Dad. Thank you for all your continued love and support. You helped "kickstart" the book by funding the location scouting tour of New York to help bring the project to life. I can't thank my "official photographer" enough for walking the equivalent of three marathons in three days as we hunted for locations in Manhattan. Your keen eye for detail has captured some amazing images.

Thanks to Ashlee for letting me crash on her couch and to her and Margaret for showing me around the Big Apple.

Finally thanks to Phil de Semlyen for providing the foreword, my sister Shona, my friends plus Katie and all the Forumites who were generous with their time to read and provide feedback during the course of writing this book.

Foreword

"It's where Harry met Sally, ghosts were busted and Rosemary had her baby. Woody Allen and John McClane call it home, and Godzilla met his end here. New York is a movie map-book waiting to happen and thanks to Dallas' keenly-observed location guide, it's happened. The camera has had a life-long love affair with Gotham's neon playgrounds, brooding alleys and glittering lights, and Ext. New York City makes the glorious trip from one side of it to the other, taking in everything from Spidey's home turf to Travis Bickle's rainy streets, via Katz's Deli and Birdman's Times Square. It's a heck of a ride."

Phil de Semlyen, Empire Magazine

Dallas King

Introduction

"Chapter One. He adored New York City. He idolised it all out proportion. No make that, he romanticised it all out of proportion. Better. To him, no matter what the season was, this was still a town that existed in black and white and pulsated to the great tunes of George Gershwin. Uh no, let me start over..."

Woody Allen and Diane Keaton sitting on a bench looking out towards the Queensboro Bridge. Audrey Hepburn, wearing those big sunglasses and party dress, seen nibbling on a pastry reflected in the window at Tiffany's at 6am. Marilyn Monroe fighting a losing battle with her skirt against a gust of wind from a subway train and even the Seventh Wonder Of The World King Kong swotting bi-planes out of the sky atop the Empire State Building.

Some of the most memorable images ever committed to celluloid and what do they all have in common?

New York City. NYC. The Big Apple. The city so nice they named it twice.

They were all filmed on location in New York City... alright, technically the last one is debatable but still, you get the point...

The old song goes *"Hooray for Hollywood"*, with Hollywoodland building its reputation for being the home of filmmaking with the studio system following the invention of the 'talkies'. Ever since location filming returned to the Big Apple in 1948 with *The Naked City* however, there is not a city in the world that has been better represented or provided more iconic imagery to the medium of film and television than New York City.

Nowadays NYC, and in particular the borough of Manhattan, is one giant backlot, playing host to dozens of television shows and movie productions on any given day.

From classic locations to new productions, there is so much for a film fan to see and experience in the "city that never sleeps" that it can be difficult to know where to start.

Ext. New York City

As the famous song in *On The Town* goes *"New York, New York, it's a wonderful town. The Bronx is up and the Battery's down..."*

This guide will provide a more in-depth, logical and efficient tour of the city than the three sailors took on their one day of shore leave in the Big Apple, whilst also looking at the evolution of film in the city.

In 2014 comedy *They Came Together*, like so many movies that came before it, New York City plays such a pivotal role in the story that there is a running joke where *"it is almost like another character"*... and it is a city full of character, and characters. One that you can come to visit in person and discover, experience and relive some of your favourite movie moments with.

You can start the day having Breakfast At Tiffany's, pay a visit to the *Ghostbusters* Firehouse, have an orgasm over lunch at Katz's Deli, all before getting a taxi ride from Travis Bickle to the Empire State Building to propose to the love of your life... or rescue her from the clutches of a giant ape!

In *Manhattan*, Woody Allen's character remarks *"Boy this really is a great city. I don't care what anybody else says. It's really a knockout you know."*

After you have spent some time in it, you'll find it hard to disagree.

Washington Street, Brooklyn

Top Ten Films: The Naked City (1948)

"There are eight million stories in the naked city. This has been one of them." – Narrator

The Naked City was one of the first films to take full advantage of the size and diversity of the Big Apple.

It was the brainchild of producer (and native New Yorker) Mark Hellinger. Hellinger sadly died of a heart attack shortly before it was screened in cinemas. However he remains part of the film as he provided the voice of the narrator. Opening the film he tells the audience that the film is *"quite different from anything you've ever seen"* and that was certainly true at the time of its release in 1948.

At that time, the majority of films were being produced in Hollywood under the studio system, often recreating other cities on their backlots, but *The Naked City* was filmed entirely on location in New York City.

It begins with a documentary feel, helped by Hellinger's narration, as the camera drifts over the city. It watches people as they go about their daily routines with New Yorkers and buildings wakening up for another day's business in the big city, until the camera comes to rest and focus on one window of an apartment building in the Upper West Side.

Inside, a young woman called Jean Dexter has just been murdered by two men.

The film evolves into a detective story, as police officers Muldoon and Halloran begin an investigation into the murder. One that will take them all over the city as they encounter a number of suspicious and duplicitous characters along the way.

The film might not have had any big names in terms of actors but that did not matter because its main star attraction was the city itself. It would receive critical acclaim at the Oscars, winning Academy Awards for its editing and cinematography.

Ext. New York City

Nowhere is this more deserved than in the film's climax in which one of the killers engages the police in a deadly shootout along the Williamsburg Bridge.

Williamsburg Bridge

Jean Dexter's Apartment - 46 W 83rd St, Upper West Side, NY 10024
Metro Station: 81 St–Museum of Natural History

Rivington Street
Metro Station: Delancey St

Williamsburg Bridge
Metro Station: Delancey St

Dallas King

Top Ten Locations: The Empire State Building

"The Empire State Building is the closest thing to heaven in this city" – An Affair To Remember

Named after the nickname for New York, the "Empire State" is the most iconic and recognisable building in New York City, if not the world. At the time of its completion in 1931, it was the tallest building in New York and its stunning Art Deco design meant that it was dubbed one of the Seven Wonders Of The Modern World.

It has featured heavily in films set in New York. From a simple establishing shot of the city to a more central role as a location in the story e.g. the elevators in *Percy Jackson And The Lightning Thief*, the offices where Buddy's dad works in *Elf* or the observation decks in *On The Town*, the Empire State Building knows how to take centre stage.

Ext. New York City

The Observation Decks are located on the 86th and 102nd floors and are open 365 days a year. They offer stunning views of the city and are a popular spot for marriage proposals. You can purchase tickets for the 86th floor, 86th & 102nd floors and pay a premium to skip the queues (depending on what time of day you visit, these could be as long as the building is tall).

King Kong (1933)

If you were to run a poll asking people for one image of New York from the movies, chances are the number one position would be taken by the sight of a giant ape atop the Empire State Building from Merlan C. Cooper's 1933 version of *King Kong*. Audiences at the time had never seen anything like it on screen before. It retains its power to this day, even when other films have tried to top it or replicate it e.g. Peter Jackson's version from 2005. The climax of both films took place at the peak of 350 5th Avenue yet neither movie actually filmed on location… for obvious reasons. The 30's film used models while Jackson used CGI and motion capture to create the effects and the Empire State.

An Affair To Remember (1957)

In this classic romance, two Manhattan socialites played by Cary Grant and Deborah Kerr meet and fall in love on board a Mediterranean cruise liner, despite being involved with other people. Upon their return to New York, they agree to meet in six months time at the top of the Empire State Building, giving them time to get their affairs in order. Do they meet? Well, you'll just have to watch the film for yourself to find out.

Sleepless In Seattle (1992)

The majority of the film takes place in Seattle however the final act takes place in New York. Divorced dad Tom Hanks and Meg Ryan, a journalist who writes to him after hearing him on a late night radio show, meet for the first time at the top of the Empire State Building with Ryan suggesting it as a meeting place after watching… you guessed it… *An Affair To Remember*.

The Empire State Building
350 5th Avenue, NY 10118
Metro Station: 34th St – Herald Square
www.esbnyc.com

Dallas King

Apocalypse New... York

As one of the most recognisable cities in the world, it will not come as much of a surprise to see New York become the focus and target of a variety of apocalyptic cinematic events ranging from natural disasters to alien invasion.

New York under siege always generates striking and memorable images (especially given the advances in computer generated effects). Whether that be an iconic landmark like the Empire State Building being blown up in *Independence Day*, an asteroid crashing into Grand Central Terminal in *Armageddon* or a lone figure wandering through the deserted remains of Times Square in I *Am Legend* (which featured a future-predicting poster advertising a *Batman vs Superman* movie).

It would be fair to say that the disaster movie in New York has taken on a different look and feel post 9/11. *War Of The Worlds* (*2005*) and *Cloverfield* contain images of ashen-covered survivors wandering shocked and confused around the city. Mindless destruction has been reduced in favour of a greater sense of responsibility for those involved. For example in *The Avengers*, a huge emphasis is placed on keeping casualties to a minimum, a lesson that could be learned by other movies such as *Man Of Steel*.

Escape From New York (1981)

In John Carpenter's sci-fi actioner, crime had become so bad in the USA that the island of Manhattan had been turned into a maximum security prison. When Air Force One crashes on the island, Kurt Russell's Snake Pliskken must go in to rescue the President.

Several iconic locations feature in the film such as Grand Central Terminal and the Public Library but the only filming to take place in New York was on Liberty Island. The rest of it was shot in St. Louis, Missouri.

The famous poster image of the severed head of the Statue of Liberty never featured in the film and it would be 27 years before it became a reality in *Cloverfield*.

Ext. New York City

The Day After Tomorrow (2004)

When the northern part of the USA finds itself in the grip of a second ice age, the focal point becomes a group of survivors who have taken refuge inside the New York Public Library.

I Am Legend (2007)

Based on the novel by Richard Matheson, Will Smith plays Robert Neville, a scientist living in a Manhattan devoid of human life. Extensive CGI was used to remove people and traffic from shots in order to effectively give off the impression of a deserted city. Several locations were completely shut off to civilians including Grand Central Approach, Washington Square Park and, at a cost of over $5 million for a six night shoot, Brooklyn Bridge.

While New Yorkers are used to filming locations popping up all over the city, filming of this scale led to some unhappy citizens and they were not afraid of voicing their annoyance. Smith himself remarked *"I don't think anyone's going to be able to do that in New York again anytime soon. People were not happy. That's the most middle fingers I've got in my career".*

Dallas King

Top Ten Films: Sweet Smell Of Success (1957)

"I love this dirty town" – J.J. Hunsecker

One of the very best films set in New York. Much of its amoral gaze can be credited to Scottish director Alexander McKendrick who brought an impartial outsider's view to the city that never sleeps… because it might get a pillow over the face from Sidney Falco, an unscrupulous press agent who would do just about anything to get ahead.

The film might be called *Sweet Smell Of Success* but the taste of it is anything but. How could it be with such acidic lines of dialogue as *"I wouldn't want to take a bite out of you Sidney. You're a cookie full of arsenic"*.

Easily the darkest and most bitter of the Hollywood films examining the cutthroat world of what happens behind the stage curtains of Broadway.

Falco (Tony Curtis), is desperate to impress New York's most influential arts columnist J.J. Hunsecker (played with a cutting relish by Burt Lancaster), a man whose very word (or lack thereof) can mean *"a man has just been sentenced to death"*, and agrees to manipulate the end of J.J.'s sister's engagement to a young musician.

Executing their plan like a couple of chess-masters, each move and countermove is met with dialogue from Ernest Lehmann and Clifford Odetts that stings like a jab to the gut e.g. *"Maybe I left my sense of humour in my other suit"* or *"Don't remove the gangplank Sidney, you might want to get back onboard"*.

Men like J.J. and Sidney operate best under the cover of darkness and neither of them would feel out of place propping up the counter in Edward Hopper's Nighthawks painting. As a result, the majority of the film is set at night with the neon of Times Square or a table lamp at the fashionable 21 Club used to illuminate one of the character's two faces.

Ext. New York City

J.J. and Susie Hunsecker's Apartment Building
The Brill Building. 1619 Broadway, NY 10019. Metro Station: 50 St

21 Club
21 W 52nd St, NY 10019. Metro Station: 5 Av-53 St
See Restaurants chapter for more details on this location

Times Square
Metro Station: Times Square–42 St
See Times Square chapter for more details on this location

Top Ten Locations: Times Square

New York City is often called "the city that never sleeps" and this is certainly true for anyone who has ever stayed in Times Square because it is Piccadilly Circus on steroids. Nicknamed the "crossroads of the world" (or even worlds as the portal that connects the Disney land of Andalasia in *Enchanted* to our reality lies beneath a manhole cover around 45th and Broadway), Times Square is a sensory overload of neon and noise.

Located in the heart of the Theatre District, it is always teeming with tourists. However this was not always the case. Originally called Longacre Square, it became Times Square when the New York Times set up headquarters here in 1904 (in the building which now houses Walgreens). In fact they threw themselves a little party to celebrate on December 31st which went on to become the world famous New Year's Eve Ball Drop.

In the Sixties and Seventies it became populated with sex shops and pornography cinemas, the type of place where Travis Bickle would take a first date and where the animals come out at night.

The 80s and 90s saw it go through a regeneration process including a large proportion of the area becoming pedestrianised. With the New York Police Department (NYPD) station at its centre, the crime rate plummeted and the

Ext. New York City

Rated-X establishments were replaced with retail and restaurants that brought with them tourists and trade.

Bob Dylan sang "*The Times They Are A-Changin*" and nowhere is that more apparent than in Times Square. No wonder that Marvel used the location for the end of *Captain America: The First Avenger* to show Steve Rogers that New York (and the world) had changed while he'd been asleep for seventy years.

Vanilla Sky (2001)

Cameron Crowe provided us with one of the most striking images of New York ever committed to film when Tom Cruise performed his trademark running through a completely empty Times Square. Incredibly this was not done using CGI but the star power of Cruise, with the production able to close off Times Square in the early hours of a Sunday morning in November 2000 to film this amazing dream sequence.

New Year's Eve (2011)

At the other end of the spectrum, one million people descend upon Times Square every December 31st to witness the legendary ball drop and ring in the New Year. Albeit that 999,999 of them are not from New York with most Manhattanites (is that even a word?) preferring to avoid the crowds. The film has several different storylines running through it, with many of them converging onto Times Square where Hilary Swank's ball drop controller is forced to deal with an undescended ball that must be fixed before midnight.

Birdman (The Unexpected Virtue Of Ignorance) (2014)

When Riggan Thomson steps outside for a mid-show cigarette to calm his nerves, he finds himself locked outside with his robe stuck in the stage door. To re-enter the theatre via the front door he is forced to walk past thousands of people in Times Square wearing just his underpants. To their utmost credit, Alejandro Inarritu and Michael Keaton achieved this shot without shutting down the area, instead shooting it guerilla-style and using a drumming group to distract the majority of the public while they got the required footage.

Times Square
Manhattan, New York
Metro Station: 42 St-Times Square

Dallas King

Broadway

"When I dreamed of Broadway, I never pictured the elk antlers" – Birdman

It might be the name of a street which stretches the entire length of Manhattan Island but, for most people, the word "Broadway" will conjure up images of the bustling Theatre District around Times Square and impromptu renditions of songs from *Les Miserables*. No trip to New York City is complete without taking in a Broadway show.

To see a "Broadway" show, technically you need to see a production in a theatre with 500+ seats. A theatre with 100-499 seats is considered "Off-Broadway".

Whatever you choose to see, if you haven't booked in advance (and if you have your heart set on specific show you really should have), the best place to pick up discounted tickets on the day is at the TKTS booth in the heart of Times Square.

At the moment, Broadway and the movie world are at the peak of a very symbiotic relationship. For many years it would be Hollywood making adaptations of successful musicals such as *West Side Story*, *Cabaret* and *Mamma Mia* but now Broadway has turned to Hollywood for source materials and is creating shows based on films like *Dirty Dancing*, *Kinky Boots* and any Disney property.

It is not all "take, take, take" with many great films having been produced about Broadway. Whether they are full-blown singing and dancing celebrations like *42nd Street* or scathing satires like *All About Eve*, *Sweet Smell Of Success* and *The Producers* (a film which was turned into a successful musical which in turn became a Hollywood movie).

It is not just the material that has appeared on stage but also the talent. In recent years, a surge of Hollywood stars have taken to treading the boards as it is every actor's dream to appear on Broadway (just ask any waiter or waitress who serves you in Midtown).

In the recent Oscar-winner *Birdman*, an actor most famous for playing a superhero attempts to make a comeback by writing and directing his own

Ext. New York City

Broadway show. However most of the actors appearing on stage at the moment are at the height of their success, with many taking a break from films to work on a play or musical. The past couple of seasons have seen A Listers and Oscar nominees like Bradley Cooper, Jake Gyllenhaal, Hugh Jackman and Emma Stone take to the stage.

If you fancy getting an autograph or selfie with your favourite celebrity, you don't have to chase them around Times Square in their underwear because many of them are happy to sign Playbills (the official free programme given away at every show) at the stage door following the performance, where the queues are handled in a well-behaved and orderly fashion. Don't bring along movie merchandise as it is normally only official show materials that will be signed.

St. James Theater – *Birdman (Or The Unexpected Virtue Of Ignorance)*
246 W 44th St, NY 10036. Metro Station: Times Square–42 St

With the majority of this Oscar-winner taking place within the confines of the theatre, director Inarritu actually reconstructed the interior on a soundstage, making subtle differences to allow for the unique form of shooting that created the illusion of the film unfolding within a single take. Film fans might notice the carpet in the backstage area bears an uncanny resemblance to that of The Overlook Hotel in *The Shining*.

Sardi's Restaurant – *The Producers/The Muppets Take Manhattan*
234 W 44th St, NY 10036. Metro Station: Times Square–42 St

In *Muppets Take Manhattan*, Kermit attempts to secure funding for a show by pretending he is a Broadway bigshot by putting his portrait on the wall, at the expense of Liza Minelli's. His plan works up to the point that the real Liza Minelli comes in and queries where her picture has gone.

John Golden Theater – *All About Eve*
252 W 45th St, NY 10036. Metro Station: Times Square–42 St

Arguably the greatest film ever made about the theatre. It is at the stage door of the John Golden Theatre that devoted fan Eve Harrington is first granted access to her idol Margo Channing, beginning a relationship that will ultimately become *All About Eve*.

Dallas King

Top Ten Films: Breakfast At Tiffany's (1961)

"Well, when I get it [the reds] the only thing that does any good is to jump in a cab and go to Tiffany's. Calms me down right away. The quietness and the proud look of it; nothing very bad could happen to you there." – Holly Golightly

When discussing films set in New York it is impossible to exclude *Breakfast At Tiffany's*. Not for the quality of the film however, which could be up for debate. For in spite of the changes to Truman Capote's original story, with the decision to cast Audrey Hepburn instead of Marilyn Monroe and Mickey Rooney's portrayal of "Japanese" tenant Mr. Yunioshi, the movie has lived on in memory as one of the most stylish movies set in New York.

Everything from the poster to Audrey Hepburn's black cocktail dress give off an air of class and elegance. One that perhaps masks the true nature of the city and the characters.

At heart *Breakfast At Tiffany's* is a love story. A love story where a hopeless romantic falls for a hard-hearted cynic who will do absolutely anything to get the lifestyle they believe they are entitled to. The life that the wonder of New York promised them.

The only difference here is that in this story it is Paul Varjak that is the romantic and Holly Golightly is the cynic.

Let's speak plainly. Despite the warm, ditzy performance of Hepburn in the film, Holly is a call girl, using her charms and skills to climb up the social ladder.

Ultimately, it is a film about loneliness. About being alone in a city of eight million people because you are unable or unwilling to take a chance and make a real connection.

In some ways Michael Fassbender's character Brandon in *Shame* is the modern male equivalent of Holly Golightly.

Here is a woman who spends her time in bars and clubs, getting $50 for the "powder" room, and window shopping at Tiffany's. Once she meets Paul, he broadens her horizons, showing her parts of New York she'd never seen before and that there is beauty in the unknown…even if it is pouring with rain.

Ext. New York City

Holly Golightly's Apartment Building
169 E 71st St, NY 10021. Metro Station: 68 St-Hunter College

This location posed as the exterior of Holly and Paul's apartment building. The interiors were all shot in a studio back in Hollywood. Before you go househunting in the Upper East Side, keep in mind that the studio set for Holly's apartment is much bigger than you would get in the traditional Brownstone style building on 71st Street!

Tiffany's
731 5th Avenue, NY 10022. Metro Station: 5 Av-59 St

Wanting to buy something from Tiffany's, Holly and Paul end up getting a crackerjack box ring engraved. The store opened on a Sunday for the very first time to allow access to film this scene.

New York Public Library
476 5th Avenue, NY 10018. Metro Station: 42 St-Bryant Park

During their day of doing things they have never done before, Holly and Paul visit the library to check out Paul's book of vignettes, Nine Lives.

Dallas King

Top Ten Locations: The Statue Of Liberty

"Magnificent isn't she? I first saw her in 1949. America was going to be the land of tolerance. Peace" – X-Men

When it comes to the Big Apple, there is only one leading lady on the big screen... and it isn't Holly Golightly.

The Statue Of Liberty was designed by Frederic Auguste Bartholdi as a gift to the United States from the people of France. She has stood tall in New York Harbour since 1886, acting as a beacon of hope and freedom to those arriving, seeking shelter or in search of the American Dream. In the sonnet The New Colussus, Emma Lazarus described her as commanding:

Ext. New York City

"Give me your tired, your poor, your huddled masses yearning to breathe free, the wretched refuse of your teeming shore. Send these, the homeless, tempest-tost to me. I lift my lamp besides the golden door."

Among the cinematic souls welcomed by Lady Liberty are *Titanic* survivor Rose Dewitt-Bukater, *Godfather*-to-be Vito Corleone and Melanie Griffith's *Working Girl*, fresh off the boat (well the Staten Island Ferry) to make it in the big city.

In real life, all that America's Great Lady has had to contend with is the odd closure for security reasons or repairs for the gradual wear-and-tear you receive as one of the world's most famous landmarks and tourist attractions. But it is precisely this iconicity that has led it to feature so heavily in the disaster and science fiction genres.

It would be difficult to argue that The Statue Of Liberty's most famous appearance on the big screen could be anything other than her reveal at the end of 1968's *Planet Of The Apes*.

It is one of the most memorable movie endings of all-time, with Charlton Heston on his knees in the sand cursing that they *"blew it all up"* as he looks at the half-buried statue, with the realisation that the eponymous Planet is in fact the future Earth. The image proved so iconic that it now appears on the posters and DVD covers, which is a shame as it essentially spoils one of cinema's greatest twists.

Since 1968, Lady Liberty has been the target for destruction for aliens (*Independence Day*, *Oblivion*), natural disasters (*Deep Impact*, *The Day After Tomorrow*) and rampaging monsters (*Cloverfield*).

In fact in 1979, Robert Holdstock predicted Hollywood's trend for fascination with the landmark:

"Where would science fiction be without the Statue of Liberty? For decades it has towered or crumbled above the wastelands of deserted Earth – giants have uprooted it, aliens have found it curious... the symbol of Liberty, of optimism, has become a symbol of science fiction's pessimistic view of the future."

But that is in the realm of science fiction and the future. For the immediate present, the Statue remains a beacon of hope and optimism, epitomised quite literally in *Ghostbusters II* when it is brought to life to inspire goodwill within the people of New York.

Saboteur (1942)

Long before he gave us the unforgettable image of Cary Grant and Eve Marie Saint hanging on for dear life off the side of Mount Rushmore in *North By Northwest*, Hitchcock used another famous landmark in one of his thriller's climaxes. Accused of starting a fire in an airplane factory, Harry Kane is forced to go on the run to clear his name. Finally tracking down the real saboteur to Liberty Island, they face off atop the Lady's torch.

Ghostbusters II (1989)

"We need something that everyone in this town can get behind. We need... a symbol. Something that appeals to the best in each of us. Something good. Something decent. Something pure."

Desperate to stop the reincarnation of an evil spirit within the body of Dana Barrett's child, the Ghostbusters must gain access to a building encased in a mood slime that feeds on the negative energy in New York City. In search of an image that will provoke feelings of hope and goodwill, they turn to the Statue of Liberty and, using positively charged slime, bring the statue to life and march her up Broadway to the tune of *Higher and Higher* by Jackie Wilson.

X-Men (2000)

The Statue Of Liberty has always been seen as a welcoming figure, but in this superhero film, mutants are not accepted by society, looked at with fear and aggression for being different. In the film's climax, Magneto attempts to turn the world's leaders into mutants using a device enclosed within Lady Liberty's torch but the X-Men turn up to thwart his evil scheme.

Statue Of Liberty
Liberty Island
Metro Station: Whitehall Street – Staten Island Ferry
www.nps.gov/stli

Ext. New York City

Martin Scorsese

"If I can make it there, I'll make it anywhere. It's up to you New York, New York"

Lyrics from one of the most famous songs of all-time, made popular by Frank Sinatra, but a song that first appeared in the 1977 film *New York, New York* which was directed by Martin Scorsese.

One of the greatest directors in the world, Scorsese really made a name for himself with his films set in New York City.

Born and raised in Little Italy, Scorsese's cinematic relationship with the city is only second to his most famous and successful partnership with Robert DeNiro. The three of them have collaborated a total of six times.

Out of his twenty three non-documentary feature films, twelve of them have been set in NYC. These range from showcasing different sides of nineteenth century New York in *The Age Of Innocence* and *Gangs Of New York*, through the *Mean Streets* of the 1970s to the wild excess of the Eighties boom in *The Wolf Of Wall Street*.

1. ***Taxi Driver (1976)***

    A mentally unstable taxi driver, who possesses a twisted perspective of the sleaze and filth that fills New York, decides to take his own form of vigilante action to clean up the streets.
    See next chapter for full details on this film.

2. ***Goodfellas (1990)***

    Based on the true story of Henry Hill and his rise and subsequent fall from grace within the New York Mob.
    At 10 E 60th St is the former site of the Copacabana club, where Marty filmed that incredible tracking shot from outside, down through the kitchen into the main room.

Dallas King

10 E 60th St

3. ***The King Of Comedy (1982)***

   Rupert Pupkin dreams of being a successful New York stand-up comic and goes to great lengths to achieve success, including stalking a chat show host he believes will give him his big break.

4. ***After Hours (1985)***

   A New York office worker has a *"very strange night"* when he meets up with a woman in a coffee shop in Soho, leading to series of bizarre and unfortunate events.

5. ***The Wolf Of Wall Street (2014)***

   A fast and frenzied look at the life of Long Island penny stockbroker Jordan Belfort who, in a parallel to Henry Hill's mobster, had a meteoric rise and fall on the ladder of success in the corporate finance world.

Ext. New York City

Top Ten Films: Taxi Driver (1976)

"All the animals come out at night – whores, skunk pussies, buggers, queens, fairies, dopers, junkies, sick, venal. Someday a real rain will come and wash all the scum off the streets. I go all over. I take people to the Bronx, Brooklyn, I take 'em to Harlem. I don't care. Don't make no difference to me."

Arguably the most controversial movie to appear on this list, *Taxi Driver* was met with shock at the time of its release over the violent content of the film's climax and the plot-line involving Jodie Foster as a 13 year-old prostitute, but is now considered to be one of the greatest films ever made.

The film would put one of New York's most iconic sights in the spotlight. Not the Empire State Building or Statue Of Liberty but the Yellow Taxi Cab.

Walking around New York City, hundreds (if not thousands) of cabs pass by you every single day. Scorsese takes this everyday item, something many New Yorkers will take for granted, and turns it into one of the main characters.

Over the course of the film, dependent on where it is and who is inside, the familiar yellow taxi cab can take on many different forms.

It can be a reassuring, dependable friend. There at a moment's notice to take you to safety. Or it can be an eerie, foreign place that is full of danger and mystery.

With Travis at the wheel, it is a vessel in which to navigate your way through the scum on the streets.

Travis discusses this with Senator Palantine in the back of his taxi, telling him that they need to "clean up this city", something that would eventually be achieved in the Nineties.

But is Travis all that different from the other animals that he hates so much?

After all, he wins the award for Most Awkward First Date in Movie History by taking Betsy (Cybill Shepherd) to a dirty movie!

The Lyric Theater
213 W 42nd St, NY 10036. Metro Station: Times Square-42 St

Now a Broadway theatre, this used to be a cinema. Specifically the porno cinema where Travis takes Betsy to see *Sometime Sweet Susan*.

USS Maine National Monument
Columbus Circle, 10023. Metro Station: Columbus Circle-59 St

Travis, sporting his brand new mohawk, plans to assassinate Senator Palantine during his campaign speech at the statue but runs off after being spotted by security personnel.

Sport's Brothel
204 & 226 E 13th St, NY 10003. Metro Station: 3 Av

When Travis finally decides to clean up the streets himself, he heads to East 13th Street. 204 is the doorway where Sport (played by Harvey Keitel) is shot by Travis and 226 is the outside of the building where Iris works as a prostitute.

204 E 13th St

Ext. New York City

Top Ten Locations: Grand Central Terminal

Grand Central Terminal has been the world's largest and busiest train station since it opened in 1913 with its 44 platforms serving 67 tracks which allow for over 500,000 commuters to pass through here every day.

Often referred to as "Grand Central Station", this is actually incorrect as it was the name of the previous station on the same site, the Grand Central & 42nd St subway station, and the name of the U.S. Post Office station building located next door.

The 44 platforms are split over two levels, or concourses. The Main Concourse is the main reason that Grand Central Terminal is one of the most popular tourist attractions in the city, with its stunning architecture an awe-inspiring sight.

In the centre of the concourse lies the main information booth that features a four-faced clock that can be seen from every point making it the perfect meeting place.

Once you are there, look up in wonder at the ceiling. An incredibly elaborate design that is astronomical in detail, scale and content as it depicts the stars and constellations of our skies.

The lower concourse is known as The Dining Concourse and, as well as 26 platforms, houses a variety of eateries including the famous Grand Central Oyster Bar.

Films that feature scenes shot in and around Grand Central include *I Am Legend*, *The Avengers*, *North By Northwest* and recently *A New York Winter's Tale*.

The Fisher King (1991)

When Robin Williams's character sees Lydia (played by Amanda Plummer) across a crowded concourse in Grand Central he attempts to speak to her but finds that their paths are blocked when the commuters swap their fast paced walking for waltzing as the Terminal becomes a fantasy ballroom.

Revolutionary Road (2008)

In Sam Mendes's adaptation of Peter Yates's Fifties-set novel, Leonardo DiCaprio and Kate Winslet play a couple living in the Connecticut suburbia but Leo's Frank Wheeler works in Manhattan and makes the daily commute into the city along with thousands of others, arriving at Grand Central Terminal.

Friends With Benefits (2011)

All good rom-coms end with an over-the-top gesture of love and/or apology and this is no different. In a slight riff on *The Fisher King*, with Mila Kunis waiting at Grand Central, Justin Timberlake organises a flash mob to the tune of "*Closing Time*" by Semisonic in order to declare his love for her and the two "friends with benefits" finally become boyfriend and girlfriend... apologies for the spoiler!

Grand Central Terminal
Manhattan, New York
Metro Station: Grand Central-42 St
www.grandcentralterminal.com

Ext. New York City

Woody Allen

It could be argued that, like the character of Alvy Singer in *Annie Hall*, Woody Allen functions best when he is in New York City. It has been the inspiration for his greatest achievements, with thirty out of his fifty feature films so far as director set in New York.

Born in Brooklyn in 1935, Allen got his break into show business by writing jokes for a local newspaper. This led to stand up comedy followed by the opportunity to write for movies. Upset with other people mishandling his material, he decided to gain full control over his projects, which has led to him becoming one of the most consistently productive filmmakers in the world, writing and directing at least one feature film a year since 1982.

For those looking to get the full Woody Allen experience during their trip to New York, if you can afford the $180 cover charge + $150 minimum spend for a table of two, then stop by Café Carlyle at The Carlyle Hotel on a Monday night where Woody Allen plays clarinet with the Eddy Davis New Orleans Jazz Band.

The Carlyle Hotel

1. *Manhattan (1979)*

   See next chapter for full details.

2. *Annie Hall (1977)*

   Neurotic comedian Alvy Singer looks back over his relationship with ditzy singer Annie Hall.

3. *Bullets Over Broadway (1994)*

   In 1920's New York, an idealistic playwright finances his new drama with money from a mobster which comes with an increasing number of editorial demands, including casting the mobster's talentless girlfriend in a leading role.

4. *Manhattan Murder Mystery (1993)*

   A middle aged couple suspect foul play when their neighbour's wife dies suddenly and set out to prove that it was murder.

5. *Broadway Danny Rose (1984)*

   Agent Danny Rose would do anything for his clients. But when he is asked to reunite a lounge singer with his mistress, Rose becomes the target of the mistress's jealous ex-boyfriend.

Ext. New York City

Top Ten Films: Manhattan (1979)

Whilst staring out over the East River from the vantage point of Sutton Place, Woody Allen's character Isaac Davis remarks:

"Boy this really is a great city, I don't care what anyone else says... it's really a knock-out you know?"

Now many would feel that this is just standard Allen dialogue, given how synonymous he is with the city, but there is more to it than that.

Up to that point, the most famous films about New York released during the Seventies were ones that exposed the seedy underbelly of the city and focused on drugs, crime, sex and violence e.g. *The French Connection, Across 110th Street, Serpico, Mean Streets* and *Taxi Driver*.

When discussing *Manhattan* with Turner Classic Movies, Allen said *"I presented a view of the city as I'd like it to be and as it can be today, if you take the trouble to walk on the right streets."*

Like the opening montage, the idea for the film *"evolved out of the music. I was listening to a record album of overtures from famous George Gershwin shows and I thought 'This would be a beautiful thing to make in black and white, you know, and make a romantic movie'."*

The result was one of Allen's most romantically optimistic movies, even ending with the now-common-place 'mad dash across town to stop the love of your life leaving town', proving that it is possible to find love in a city of 8 million people but it is also his biggest love letter to the city of New York itself.

The borough of Manhattan has rarely looked better than it has through the lens of Gordon Willis who photographed the city in beautiful widescreen monochrome, providing a stunning showcase for the location.

Allen had chosen to shoot in black and white because *"that's how I remember it from when I was small. Maybe it's a reminiscence from old photographs, films, books and all that but that's how I remember New York".*

Dallas King

Sutton Place Park
Riverview Terrace, NY 10022. Metro Station: Lexington Av-59 St

Site of that unforgettable shot of Woody Allen and Diane Keaton sitting on a bench at the East River looking out towards the Queensboro bridge. It recently got its own R-Rated pastiche in *Trainwreck*. If making a visit to this location, prepare yourselves to find no bench at that exact spot as they had to bring their own.

Zabar's
2245 Broadway, NY 10001. Metro Station: 79 St
See page 81 for more details on this location

Isaac and his seventeen year-old girlfriend played by Muriel Hemingway shop for groceries and discuss Diane Keaton's character at this NY Deli.

Museum Of Modern Art
11 W 53rd St, NY 10019. Metro Station: 5 Av/53 St

Manhattan features scenes in several museums but in this feisty exchange, the characters of Isaac and Mary are immediately at odds over their opposing views on art.

Ext. New York City

Top Ten Locations: Central Park

"Didn't your mother warn you that you shouldn't go out in Central Park at night? My mother was the reason you shouldn't go into Central Park at night!"
– Stuart Little

Despite what the film quote might imply, Central Park is one of the most serene and beautiful areas of Manhattan. It is often an oasis of calm from the hustle and bustle of the city and many New Yorkers will come here to jog, run or just sit and relax and take in the many sights and attractions within the park.

So many of these have appeared on the silver screen that this book could have concentrated on Central Park alone..

With over 350 films shot within the confines of the 843 acres that run from 59th all the way up to 110th Street, bigger than the principality of Monaco, Central Park is the most filmed location in the world.

Some of the familiar cinematic highlights include: Trump Wollman Ice Rink (*Serendipity*), Central Park Zoo (*Madagascar*), Tavern On The Green (*Wall Street*, *Ghostbusters*), The Central Park Boathouse Restaurant (*When Harry Met Sally*), Bethesda Fountain (*The Producers*), Belvedere Castle (*Two Days In New York*) and The Mall (*Definitely Maybe*).

It also houses the Metropolitan Museum Of Art and has the Natural History and Guggenheim Museums on its perimeter (see the chapter on Museums on page 82 for more information).

Kramer Vs Kramer (1979)

The Mall, the walkway that leads to Bethesda Terrace and stretches from 66th to 72nd St, is the site for both joy and sadness for Ted Kramer. It is where he teaches Billy to ride a bike but also where Billy is reunited with his mother for the first time since she left them.

Die Hard With A Vengeance (1995)

Challenged by Simon Gruber to get from 72nd Street to Wall Street in 30 minutes, John McClane decides to take a shortcut through Central Park. When passenger Zeus informs him that Park Drive is just as busy as everywhere else, McClane replies *"I didn't say Park Drive, I said through the park!"* and proceeds to take a scenic driving tour through the park, over the grass and footpaths, making it from 72nd and Broadway to Central Park South in 3 minutes in what *"must be a record"*.

Enchanted (2007)

The easiest and quickest way to see what Central Park has to offer is to watch this modern Disney fairy tale with a twist as Giselle's musical number *How Do You Know* explores the majority of the popular landmarks the park has to offer in just 4 minutes, ending at the Bethesda Fountain which also featured in both versions of *The Producers*.

If you want to retrace Giselle's footsteps, look out your most comfortable pair of shoes as it will be quite a walk and take a lot longer than a song to take in all the sights. For a little assistance on maximising your time and energy, the two hour On Location Walking Tour of Central Park is highly recommended (www.onlocationtour.com/tour/central-park-tv-movies).

Central Park
Metro Station: 5 Av-59 St
www.centralparknyc.org

Ext. New York City

Horror

It might be one of the most filmed cities in the world but one genre where NYC has perhaps not provided its fair share of iconic moments is the Horror movie.

When death and destruction come to the streets of Manhattan, it tends to be in the form of a widespread disaster or apocalyptic invasion. Displays of murder and mayhem at the hands of vampires, zombies, ghouls, goblins and serial killers are much rarer.

The success of certain genres can be cyclical in nature and linked to the tastes of the audience or even social and political circumstances. The most successful time period for New York-based horror films was in the Eighties, with many of them reflecting the uglier side of the city, areas that have since undergone regeneration. Several of them such as *Basket Case*, *Frankenhooker* and *C.H.U.D.* would contain scenes set in the pre-Mayor Rudy Giuliani Times Square.

The Dakota Building

Rosemary's Baby (1968)

Rosemary and Guy Woodhouse move into their dream apartment in a building called The Bramford but it soon becomes a nightmare when they discover they are living next to the neighbours from hell.

For filming of the exterior of the building, they used The Dakota on 72nd and Central Park West which was also Tom Cruise's apartment building in *Vanilla Sky*. In real life it was home to celebrities such as Lauren Bacall and John Lennon, who was shot and killed just outside the building. A tribute to Lennon lies just across the road in Central Park at Strawberry Fields.

Friday The 13th Part VIII: Jason Takes Manhattan (1989)

A slightly misleading and potentially disappointing title. Jason only arrives in Manhattan towards the end of the movie to wreak havoc upon Times Square. The film's climax takes place in the sewers below, where he could well have come across the cannibals from *C.H.U.D.* for movie-crossover potential.

Black Swan (2011)

Part Polanski-esque psychological horror and part "were-swan" movie, in which Natalie Portman's ballet dancer Nina slowly loses her mind when she takes on the dual role of the White and Black Swan in a production of Swan Lake. Nina's swan song performance (pun intended) takes place at the David S. Koch Theater in the Lincoln Center.

Ext. New York City

Top Ten Films: Ghostbusters (1984)

Who ya gonna call for one of the most popular films set in New York City? GHOSTBUSTERS!

In addition to saving the lives of millions of registered voters, the paranormal investigators showcased the city from a geographical standpoint, busting ghosts all the way from Chinatown to Central Park West. They also embodied the brains, heart, soul and cynicism of the Big Apple through its trio of lead characters Ray Stantz, Egon Spengler and Peter Venkman.

Whether he is being faced with an 80ft tall Marshmallow Man and remarking that *"he's a sailor in New York, we get this guy laid we don't have a problem"* or telling a government employee that he is phallically challenged, Venkman was the archetypal Eighties New York Everyman whom the city could relate to.

The film provided many iconic New York moments and they would add to them in 1989 with the sequel *Ghostbusters II*, taking in locations such as the US Customs House, Washington Square Park and The Statue Of Liberty (see page 17 for more details).

It is clear that the Ghostbusters have done a lot for New York City and it is not hard to see why once you have spent some time soaking in the "spirit" of the city. Then you, just like Winston Zedemore, will find yourself exclaiming *"I love this town!"*.

Ghostbusters Firehouse
14 North Moore Street, NY10013. Metro Station: Franklin St

Described as being situated in a *"demilitarised zone"*, the Hook and Ladder Firehouse lies in the heart of Tribeca (now home to Robert DeNiro, Jay-Z and Beyonce among other celebrities) and is the site of many a film fan pilgrimage. It still exists as a fully operational fire station and the *Ghostbusters II* sign is proudly displayed on the wall inside.

Dallas King

Ivo Shandor Building
55 Central Park West, NY 10023. Metro Station: 59 St–Columbus Circle

Sigourney Weaver's corner penthouse suite (complete with interdimensional fridge) is located at *"Spook Central"*, otherwise known as 55 Central Park West, just up the road from Columbus Circle where the Stay Puft Marshmallow Man makes his first appearance.

New York Public Library
5th Avenue & 42nd Street, NY 10018. Metro Station: Bryant Park–42 St

Location of the film's opening scene and the team's first encounter with a *"free-floating full torso vaporous apparition"*.

See the chapter on page 36 for more information on this location.

Ext. New York City

Top Ten Locations: New York Public Library

Despite what the movies or certain episodes of *Seinfeld* would have you believe, the largest branch of the New York Public Library, situated on Fifth Avenue next to Bryant Park, is not actually a lending library.

In another piece of deception, the interior of the library was used for the interior of the Metropolitan Museum Of Art in *The Thomas Crown Affair* (*1999*) when Crown uses doubles all dressed as Magritte's The Son Of Man to confuse the police as he returns a stolen painting.

Guarded by the two marble lions Patience and Fortitude, technically it is called the Stephen A. Schwarzman Building and despite being just one of 91 branches in the city, it is often referred to as *the* New York Public Library, given that it is the main branch and the largest. It houses hundreds of thousands of books in its hallowed halls and reading rooms which include the Rose Main Reading Room which is the size of an American Football field.

Ghostbusters (1984)

The film's opening scene takes place in the lower level of the library, as an elderly librarian is terrorised by an as-yet unseen ghost.

The Day After Tomorrow (2004)

When an ecological disaster plunges the Northern hemisphere into a second ice age, in New York a group of people seek shelter and refuge inside the library. Desperate to survive until they can be rescued, the group have to resort to burning furniture and even books. Here's hoping they left the classics and just used copies of *The Da Vinci Code* and *Fifty Shades Of Grey*!

Sex And The City (2008)

When Carrie returns her copy of "Great Love Letters Of Great Men" (which as previously noted is technically impossible), she finds the perfect venue for her wedding to Mr. Big. Just a shame that the ceremony didn't match the majesty of the venue.

New York Public Library
5th Avenue at 42nd Street, NY 10018
Metro Station:Bryant Park–42 St
www.nypl.org

Ext. New York City

Holidays

There is always a reason to be celebrating in New York City. After all, you are in the greatest city in the world. Americans pride themselves on throwing the biggest parties and celebration so here are a few dates for your diary where New Yorkers pull out all the stops, along with some cinematic inspiration.

Valentine's Day

New York can be one of the most romantic cities in the world, as evidenced on screen in films such as *Serendipity*, *Moonstruck*, *You've Got Mail* and *Down With Love*. There is no shortage of romantic things to do in Manhattan on Valentine's Day: from a stroll through Central Park, shopping at Tiffany's, fine dining at a restaurant, perhaps ending with a proposal at the Top of the Rock or Empire State Building.

Independence Day

America might commemorate the adoption of the Declaration of Independence on the 4th July but when it comes to the cinema, think of New York and *Independence Day* and it will conjure up images of a giant alien spaceship destroying the Empire State Building. Thankfully the only fireworks you will see in real life are on the East River at sunset in one of the city's biggest celebrations.

Halloween

The best way to experience All Hallow's Eve, asides from catching a late night horror movie at a repertory cinema, is to check out the Village Halloween Parade. Every year thousands of people in costume celebrate this holiday by parading up 6th Avenue from Spring Street to 16th Street.

Thanksgiving

One thing you simply must do before Thanksgiving dinner and queuing for Black Friday deals is witness the famous Macy's Thanksgiving Day Parade. Every year on the fourth Thursday of November, giant balloons and floats make their way from 72nd Street down to Herald Square where Macy's is situated.

The parade has featured in a number of movies including *Mistress America* and most famously *Miracle On 34th Street*.

Christmas

Miracle On 34th Street would feature very high up on any list of Best Christmas Films set in New York. One should pay a visit to Macy's at Christmas to try and catch a glimpse of Kris Kringle but if he isn't there then there are still plenty of stunning window displays to take in.

Other New York Christmas Crackers include *Elf* and *Scrooged*, a modern re-telling of Charles Dickens's A Christmas Carol starring Bill Murray.

If you are in New York for the festive season then make sure to try skating at Wollman Ice Rink or Rockefeller Center which is the site of the Tree Lighting Ceremony.

New Year's Eve

Seeing in the New Year in New York can be done one of two ways. If you are a tourist, it is in Times Square. If you live in New York, then anywhere else!

The Times Square revelry features heavily in *New Year's Eve* but other films that remind us what to do "should auld acquaintance be forgot" include *When Harry Met Sally* and *Trading Places*.

Ext. New York City

Top Ten Films: Wall Street (1985)

Oliver Stone's *Wall Street* is not merely a movie or a snapshot of a time in American history. By treating Gordon Gecko's "*Greed, for lack of a better word, is good*" as gospel, the movie became a bible or life manual for every young broker and banker who worked, or dreamed of working, in "the city".

This was not Stone's intention with the film. Initially it was designed as an expose of the world of Manhattan's financial district, with the central character of Bud Fox selling his soul to the devil for wealth, women and success before getting his comeuppance.

Unfortunately many of the people who watched the film had no soul to begin with and didn't view it as a morality tale. Instead seeing Bud's descent into hell by insider trading and securities fraud as a step-by-step guide to getting ahead. They saw the difference between Bud's tiny studio apartment and the luxury apartment he moves into in St. James Tower and said "I want that". It was then a simple step to decide that Gordon Gecko was the man to help get them there.

Admittedly Michael Douglas's Oscar-winning performance is rather persuasive. Whether he is schooling Bud Fox over steak tartare at 21 Club, even if he doesn't stay for lunch because *"lunch is for wimps"*, or delivering his infamous "Greed Is Good" speech in the ballroom of the Roosevelt Hotel, Gecko was the poster child for bankers everywhere. Both in real life and on the silver screen, inspiring the likes of Patrick Bateman in *American Psycho* and Jordan Belfort in *The Wolf Of Wall Street*.

21 Club
21 W 52nd St, NY 10019. Metro Station: 5 Av–53 St

See the Restaurants chapter for more details on this location.

St. James's Tower – Bud Fox's Apartment Building
415 E 54th St, NY 10022. Metro Station: Lexington Av–53 St

New York County Supreme Court House
60 Centre St, NY 10007. Metro Station: Brooklyn Bridge–City Hall/Chambers St

Ext. New York City

Top Ten Locations: Rockefeller Center

In terms of a filming location, the Rockefeller Center is more widely known for television than film, as it is the home of NBC Studios who host *The Tonight Show with Jimmy Fallon* and *Saturday Night Live* as well as being the setting for *30 Rock*, which is the building's nickname.

Rockefeller Center is named after John D. Rockefeller who privately financed and developed the project in 1930. The site of Rockefeller Plaza houses several buildings and spans 48th to 51st Street between 5th and 6th Avenue.

The highlight is 30 Rockefeller Plaza which houses The Top Of The Rock observation area and was the site of the famous 'Lunchtime atop a skyscraper' photo taken by Charles C. Ebbets during the building's construction.

Back on solid ground, the rest of the plaza contains several prime retail establishments, office space, a dining concourse, NBC Studios and Radio City Music Hall.

Radio City Music Hall opened in 1932 and for a long time was the destination for movie premieres in New York, with a stunning auditorium capable of seating up to 5933 people. These days it is a venue for concerts and stage shows including the widely popular Radio City Christmas Spectacular starring The Rockettes.

As a filming location, Rockefeller Plaza might not be as widely used as others in Manhattan but it is almost guaranteed to make an appearance (albeit brief) in any film set in New York at Christmas time. The plaza will appear in establishing shots of the festive season due to it having the biggest Christmas tree in the city and the very popular ice rink.

Ext. New York City

Saboteur (1942)

A Hitchcockian villain attempts to evade the authorities at Rockefeller Center by slipping through the crowded audience watching a movie in Radio City Music Hall but instead triggers a deadly shootout.

Radio Days (1987)

In a scene where the lead character goes to see a movie at Radio City Music Hall during the heyday of radio, the narrator comments "It was the first time I'd ever seen the Radio City Music Hall and it was like entering heaven. I just never saw anything so beautiful in my life".

The Adjustment Bureau (2010)

Despite the best efforts of the bureau to keep them apart, star-crossed lovers David and Elise make one last desperate plea to be allowed to stay together at the Top Of The Rock.

Rockefeller Center
Rockefeller Plaza
Metro Station: 47-50 Sts/Rockefeller Center
www.rockefellercenter.com

Dallas King

Sex In The City

New York City is no stranger to romance. After all, this is the city in which the likes of Tom Hanks, Meg Ryan, Audrey Hepburn and Cary Grant have found love. It is a comforting feeling to watch two people fall in love in the Big Apple on the big screen. After all, if you can find that special someone in a city of eight million people then there is hope for all of us right?

But what happens when the credits roll? What happens once the couple have got their "happy ever after"?

We're all adults here. Let's face it, they will be off consummating the relationship. It is a natural, normal thing for two adults to do but the attitude to sex on screen has always been slightly more prudish. In a rather extreme example, in the horror genre, sex = death.

In the Eighties, accompanying the mood of the time and the city, sex was seen as seedy, illicit and taboo, exemplified by films such as *Fatal Attraction, 9 ½ Weeks, Dressed To Kill* and *Cruising*.

However the representation of sex on screen in New York began to change towards the late Eighties and Nineties along with the attitudes of society.

A change which began with two people called Harry Burns and Sally Albright and continued with four women called Carrie, Charlotte, Miranda and Samantha. The frankness of their discussions and attitudes to sex in the HBO TV series *Sex And The City* began to filter through to the movies.

Not only did the girls get a big screen outing of their own in 2008 but it would pave the way for mainstream films about sex like *Friends With Benefits, That Awkward Moment* and the Golden Globe-nominated *Shame*.

Carrie Bradshaw's Apartment Building (*Sex And The City*)
66 Perry St, NY 10014. Metro Station: 14 St

The exterior to Carrie's rent-controlled apartment in the fashionable Greenwich Village.

Ext. New York City

66 Perry St

Michael Fassbender's Apartment Building (Shame)
9 W 31st St, NY 10001. Metro Station: 33 St

Hotel Chelsea.
222 W 23rd St, NY 10011. Metro Station: 23 St
Site of one of Mickey Rourke and Kim Basinger's trysts in *9 ½ Weeks*.

Dallas King

Top Ten Films: When Harry Met Sally (1989)

Many films have dealt with the issue but this was first film to openly ask the question:

"Can men and women be friends or does sex always get in the way?"

The answer, in this particular case, is no... well, yes... but no... then yes.

When Harry Met Sally is one of the greatest romantic comedies of all-time and feels like the best Woody Allen film he never made.

Billy Crystal is at his neurotic best in one of the most realistic portrayals of a man in the genre. This movie also kickstarted Meg Ryan's reign as the Rom-Com Queen resulting in her own New York Trilogy that also included *Sleepless In Seattle* and *You've Got Mail*.

It might have taken a long time for Harry and Sally's "Will they? Won't they?" relationship to come to fruition but one connection which was instantaneous was the film's love for New York City. Filmed in such a way that it would create a long-lasting bond with the characters and the audience.

Harry actually meets Sally when they drive from Chicago to New York City after graduating from college. Along the way, their differing views on life, love and the ending of *Casablanca* result on them deciding they wouldn't be friends. Years later they meet again on a flight leaving from New York and once again they go their separate ways.

It isn't actually until they meet face-to-face in New York in a branch of Shakespeare & Co bookstore that they finally become friends. Perhaps it is the magic of the city that helped to build this relationship.

Different areas and faces of New York were used depending on the film's plot at that time. Moments between Sally and her female friends take place in restaurants like The Loeb Boathouse in Central Park. Conversations between Harry and his male friend Jesse are set in typically male venues like a batting cage in Coney Island or the perfect comic timing of the Mr. Zero speech at a New York Giants game.

Ext. New York City

Despite being "just friends", Harry and Sally spend a lot of time in ideal "meet-cute" locations like Central Park, The Metropolitan Museum Of Art and dining out together in various restaurants, resulting in the most famous film food moment in cinema history as Sally demonstrates the art of the female orgasm over lunch at Katz's Deli.

So make sure to *"have what she's having"* by visiting some of the locations where Harry Met Sally.

Katz's Delicatessen
205 E Houston St, NY 10002. Metro Station: 2 Av

See chapter on Restaurants for more information on this location

Washington Square Park
Metro Station: 8 St–NYU

See chapter on page 49 for more information on this location.

Puck Building
295 Lafayette Street, NY 10012. Metro Station: Broadway-Lafayette Street

As Harry walks alone in New York on New Year's Eve, he passes the Washington Square Park Arch and decides that *"when you want to spend the rest of your life with someone, you want the rest of your life to start as soon as possible"* and runs to the Puck Building, so called because of the statues of the *Midsummer Night's Dream* character above the doorway, to tell Sally exactly how he feels.

Top Ten Locations: Washington Square Park

This public park is most well known for its giant arch honouring George Washington, hence the name of the park, and the large fountain located at its centre. It is also a cultural hub of Greenwich Village, where it is located at the bottom of Fifth Avenue, and you can often find it full of avid chess players, musicians and students simply taking a break from their studies at the nearby New York University campus.

When Harry Met Sally (1989)

Following an awkward drive from Chicago to New York where they debate whether of not men and women can really be friends without sex getting in the way, Harry and Sally part ways for the first time underneath the arch.

Ext. New York City

I Am Legend (2008)

When a plague decimates the population of the United States, killing millions and turning others into creatures of the night, immune scientist Robert Neville is the lone survivor on the island of Manhattan. Living in a townhouse on the corner of Washington Square Park with his companion Samantha (his dog), he spends his days scavenging for supplies and capturing the creatures to experiment on in an effort to find a cure.

Begin Again (2014)

A down-on-his-luck producer, played by Mark Ruffalo, meets singer-songwriter Keira Knightley at an open mic night and persuades her to record an open-air album, using the city as their studio. Locations include rooftops, subway stations, alleyways and beneath the arch in Washington Square Park.

Washington Square Park
Washington Square Park
Metro Station: W 4 St–Washington Sq or 8 St -NYU

Spike Lee

Spike Lee, like Woody Allen and Martin Scorsese before him, is a filmmaker whose work is synonymous with the city of New York. So it might surprise some to learn that he was actually born in Atlanta, Georgia but his family moved to Brooklyn when he was a child.

While Allen and Scorsese might focus on a certain type of New Yorker, Lee's films take in a more diverse cross section of the city.

From all the way up in the Bronx with *Summer Of Sam*, down to the financial district for *Inside Man*. Then across the East River to Brooklyn in *Do The Right Thing* and Coney Island with *He Got Game*.

In a way, Lee has similarities to one of Scorsese's characters, Travis Bickle, in that he "goes all over" New York City. Anytime, Anywhere.

1. ***Do The Right Thing (1989)***

   See next chapter for full details on this film.

2. ***25th Hour (2002)***

   A man uses his last 24 hours of freedom to put his affairs in order before starting a seven year prison sentence for drug offences. Norton's incendiary "Fuck You" monologue was the explosion of anger that the city was feeling at the time, with many citing this as the best film made about post 9/11 New York City.

Ext. New York City

World Trade Center

3. ***Jungle Fever (1991)***

Predominantly set in the Harlem and Bensonhurst areas of the city, a successful and married black architect contemplates an affair with his Italian secretary and the film looks at the impact it has on them and their relationships.

4. ***Summer Of Sam (1999)***

Lee's take on the "Son Of Sam" murders of 1977, focusing on the residents of an Italian-American neighbourhood of the Bronx as they live in fear of the serial killer prowling the streets.

5. ***Inside Man (2006)***

Sent to a oversee a bank robbery and hostage situation, an NYPD detective attempts to stop a criminal commiting the perfect crime.

Dallas King

Top Ten Films: Do The Right Thing (1989)

The majority of the films featured in this guide take place in Manhattan but New York City is made up of five boroughs including Brooklyn which is the setting for Spike Lee's third feature film as director and until that point was rather under-represented on the big screen.

What Spike Lee does well is to shine a light on people and areas of the city that arguably had not received their dues in the past.

Taking place during a summer heatwave entirely on one day and in one location, Stuyvesant Avenue, the film is a melting pot of race and temperature.

The Bed-Stuy area was originally an Italian-American neighbourhood, represented here by Sal's Pizzeria which has proudly sat on the corner of the street for 25 years, but is now the home to a predominantly African-American and Hispanic community.

On the hottest day of the year, tempers soon rise as quickly as the temperature, boiling over into a moment of violence that will change the neighbourhood forever.

This moment, when an angry mob trash Sal's Pizzeria and set it on fire, marks a turning point on the evolution of New York City on film.

With Sal's on fire, the Wall of Fame goes up in flames, among them celebrities like Al Pacino and Robert DeNiro.

Here Lee was burning down the stars of *The Godfather* and *Taxi Driver*, announcing to the world that the time of the Italian-American mob/crime movie was over and a new era in cinema was going to rise from the ashes.

Stuyvesant Avenue, Brooklyn
Nearest Metro Station: Kosciusko Street

Ext. New York City

Top Ten Locations: Brooklyn Bridge

"Sure, I know a place right across the Brooklyn Bridge where they'll never find us... Brooklyn!" – On The Town

Brooklyn Bridge is one of the four bridges connecting Manhattan Island to the East boroughs of Brooklyn, Williamsburg and Queens, the others being the Manhattan, Williamsburg and Queensboro Bridges. What imaginative names they give their bridges in NYC, no "Golden Gate" here!

Completed and opened for use on May 24th 1883, Brooklyn Bridge was the first steel-wire suspension bridge constructed and remains one of the oldest suspension bridges in the United States, becoming a National Historic Landmark in 1964.

The best way to see a city is to walk the streets and one of the best walks in New York City is to hop on the A or C train across to Brooklyn and walk back across the bridge to the financial district. Go first thing in the morning or at dusk for the best views.

Beyond its primary use as a passageway and thoroughfare, even for zombies as seen in *Zombie Flesh Eaters*, its cinematic use is threefold, as exemplified by these films.

Mo' Better Blues (1990)

Although constantly busy during the day with commuters, it is possible to find a quiet moment of solitude first thing in the morning or late at night. Something that Denzel Washington's musician takes full advantage of as he plays his trumpet at night, serenading the taxis and cars that drive by below him.

Enchanted (2007)

Its inclusion in this book is clearly testament to the fact that Brooklyn Bridge is one of the must-see experiences in NYC. It is not just busy with commuters looking to get some exercise and fresh air instead of being cooped up on the subway but it is popular with tourists. Giselle takes her Prince Charming here on their "first date", making the most of it with their Statue Of Liberty hats, hotdogs and I Heart NY paraphernalia

Cloverfield (2008)

Architecturally speaking, Brooklyn Bridge is the most photogenic bridge in the city. Unfortunately this does mean that if a bridge needs to be destroyed in a New York-set movie, nine out of ten times this will be the first one to go.

And so it is when a monster of mysterious origin rampages through the city and rips through the bridge, killing thousands of people and cutting off the escape route for the lead characters and their trusty, omnipresent camcorder.

Brooklyn Bridge
Metro Station: Brooklyn Bridge-City Hall-Chambers St (Manhattan Side) or High St–Brooklyn Bridge (Brooklyn Bridge)

Ext. New York City

Superhero City

As witnessed in the chapter on apocalyptic New York, the Big Apple can often find itself under threat and holding out for a hero.

Thankfully in the realm of comic books and their big screen adaptations, there are many superheroes who call New York City home and will fight to defend it. These include your friendly neighbourhood Spider-Man and Brooklyn's own Steve Rogers aka Captain America.

The headquarters of Marvel Comics has always been based in NYC and many of their characters also live within the five boroughs.

Part of the enduring appeal of both the comics and the characters is that even although these characters were mutants or beings with fantastical powers, they were grounded in a reality that was familiar to the readers. Seeing them interact with real-life places and situations helped to increase their relatability and popularity.

You have Peter Parker residing in Queens, Daredevil patrolling the streets of Hell's Kitchen and the Fantastic Four living and working in the Baxter Building that appears in the Manhattan Skyline.

So when it comes to adapting these stories to the big screen, the producers are lucky in that a large proportion of the location scouting, production design and even storyboarding has already been done for them by the comic book artists. Although these are not always set in stone as the key word is 'adaptations', with the makers of *The Amazing Spider-Man 2* sadly not opting to recreate the infamous cover of issue 122 for the finale of the film.

Even DC Comics, who created fictional cities for their most famous heroes Batman and Superman, have used the backlot that is New York City when it came to bringing Metropolis to life in Richard Donner's *Superman* or elements of Gotham in Christopher Nolan's *Dark Knight Trilogy*.

The current boom in comic book movies really took off with the success of *Spider-Man* in May 2002, when it became the first film to take over $100 million at the US box office in its opening weekend.

Dallas King

Following 9/11, America and New York in particular was in need of a hero and they found one in the form of a costumed superhero from their own backyard. This may partially explain the popularity of the movie at the time.

For the last twelve years Earth's mightiest heroes have defended its greatest city before coming full circle with the Battle for New York in *The Avengers* in 2012, which became the first film to earn over $200 million in its first weekend.

The city and its inhabitants are characters in their own right which adds to the stakes of the adventures, for example the NYPD who move the people to safety in *The Avengers* during the battle against the Chitauri at the behest of the embodiment of the American Dream Captain America.

Although in comics and movies superheroes have not always gained the approval of the authorities or certain editors of The Daily Bugle, they have been welcomed with open arms by the people of New York and the same goes for comic book fans, with lots for them do in the Big Apple.

Every October, the city plays host to the New York Comic Con (www.newyorkcomiccon.com), held at the Javits Convention Center. It welcomes 120,000 visitors every year over a four day period making it the largest event of its type outside of San Diego.

Recommended comic book stores include the original Midtown Comics near Times Square on 200 W 40th St & 7th Avenue, which comic book fans might recognise as the same cross section where Bernie had his newsstand in the Watchmen graphic novel. Another great store is St. Marks Comics (11 St Marks Place between 2nd & 3rd Avenue) which featured in an episode of *Sex And The City*.

For those looking to walk in the footsteps of their favourite superheroes, then Celebrity Planet's Superhero Walking Tour is highly recommended. Running every Fri/Sat/Sun at 2.00, it lasts 90 minutes and will take you on a fun, fact-filled guide through some of Midtown's most super locations. (www.celebrityplanet.com/newyork/the-superhero-tour-of-new-york.html).

Ext. New York City

The News Building – The Daily Planet (Superman (1978))
220 E 42nd St between 2nd and 3rd Avenue, NY 10017. Metro Station: Grand Central-42 St

The interior lobby and exterior of this building played the part of the offices of The Daily Planet newspaper where Superman worked undercover as Clark Kent and first met Lois Lane.

Grand Central Terminal/Pershing Square/Park Avenue – The Avengers (2012)
42nd Street. Metro Station: Grand Central-42 St.

When Loki opens a portal above Stark Tower (digitally replacing the Met Life building above Grand Central), he unleashes the Chitauri army upon Manhattan with the Avengers battling them in the area closely surrounding the Terminal building.

Queensboro Bridge – The Dark Knight Rises (2012)
Ed Koch Queensboro Bridge, NY

With NYC being used for the set of Gotham in this Batman film, when Bane takes over the city with the League Of Shadows, he blows up all the bridges and tunnels, leaving the Queensboro Bridge as the only access to the city... and the only escape route, with several scenes filmed here.

Dallas King

Top Ten Films: Spider-Man (2002)

As briefly discussed in the previous chapter, New York City was in need of a hero following the events of September 11th 2001 and it found one in the form of everyone's favourite friendly neighbourhood *Spider-Man*.

This was the first superhero film to be released after 9/11 and the first movie to gross over $100 million in its opening weekend. It was the catalyst behind the revitalisation of the comic book genre that had threatened to flatline following the failure of *Batman and Robin*. It started the wave of success that is yet to break some thirteen years on.

The film was clearly influenced by the events of 9/11 as Sony Pictures had created a teaser trailer that featured a helicopter being caught in a giant web between the Twin Towers, and that was pulled after the tragedy.

It also led to an addition in a scene towards the end of the film where Spidey is trying to rescue Mary-Jane and a tram full of passengers on the Queensboro Tramway. The Green Goblin's attempts to attack Spider-Man are interrupted by New Yorkers shouting *"You mess with Spidey, you mess with New York. You mess with one of us, you mess with all of us"*.

Spider-Man is certainly the Marvel hero who gets the best views of the city, web-crawling along buildings and swinging from rooftop to rooftop.

Using a "Spidey-Cam" rig set up between buildings that could be raised and lowered as necessary, director Sam Raimi was able to achieve the effect of seeing what Spider-Man sees when swinging through the streets.

He is your friendly neighbourhood Spider-Man but Spidey doesn't restrict his heroics to his home borough of Queens. He takes in sights all over the city:

The Flatiron Building
175 5th Avenue, NY 10010. Metro Station: 23 St

In Sam Raimi's trilogy, the Flatiron building houses the offices of The Daily Bugle newspaper and their fearsome editor J. Jonah Jameson.

Ext. New York City

Flatiron Building

New York Public Library
5th Avenue at 42nd St, NY 10018. Metro Station: 5 Av

It is outside the library that Uncle Ben imparts his words of wisdom to Peter, in that *"with great power comes great responsibility"*.

Roosevelt Island Tramway
2nd Avenue, NY 10022. Metro Station: Lexington Av/59 St.

The tramway that transports people from Manhattan Island to Roosevelt Island is the site of a twisted game orchestrated by 6the Green Goblin. He forces Spider-Man to choose between saving a tram full of passengers and his beloved Mary-Jane.

Top Ten Locations: Coney Island

Despite having places like Central Park and the High Line, one can feel cooped up in the built-up urban Manhattan during the wet, hot American summers and it can leave you dreaming of an escape to sandy beaches and an ocean view.

Well, that is one dream that can come true and is closer than you might expect. For only a 50 minute subway ride from the centre of Manhattan, at the end of D, Q, N and F lines, lies Coney Island.

In movie terms, it feels like New York's very own Amity Island. Albeit one that has not suffered from shark attacks on the 4th of July.

Located at the South West corner of Brooklyn, Coney Island comes alive every summer with thousands of people visiting every day to soak up the sun on Brighton Beach, stroll along the boardwalk, catch the fireworks every Friday during the summertime and visit the amusements of Luna Park.

Ext. New York City

Luna Park (www.lunaparknyc.com), unlike the beach and boardwalk which are open all year round, is a seasonal attraction. Open from Spring to Fall during the weekends and holidays (running a full schedule during June-August), it has all sort of amusements and rides including the 88 year old wooden rollercoaster The Cyclone.

If you don't have the stomach for rollercoasters, then you might have for one of Nathan's Famous Hot Dogs. Or a few dozen more if you fancy entering the Hot Dog Eating Contest held every Independence Day.

Annie Hall (1977)

Coney Island is the birthplace of comedian Alvy Singer (Woody Allen) who grew up in a house directly underneath the Thunderbolt rollercoaster.

The location was not just inserted there for comic effect but actually did exist. The building was The Kensington Hotel but sadly it was demolished along with the rollercoaster in 2000 before a new version of the Thunderbolt was built in its place.

The Warriors (1981)

Coney Island is a sight for sore eyes for The Warriors when they finally arrive at the end of the film. Their home turf, it is where they have spent a very long night fighting to get back to, all the way from the Bronx, being hunted by every other street gang in NYC after being falsely accused of murdering a rival gang leader.

9 ½ Weeks (1986)

The mysterious John (Mickey Rourke) takes Elizabeth (Kim Basinger) on a date to Coney Island, complete with balloons and a ride on the Wonder Wheel.

Coney Island
Nearest Metro Station: Coney Island

Dallas King

Gangs Of New York

As discussed in the chapter on Horror films set in New York, the production and success of certain genres can be linked to what is happening in society at the time.

In the 70s, 80s and 90s, New York was viewed as one of the most dangerous cities in the world.

During the Nineties, a combination of the mayorship of Rudy Giulani, his predecessor David Dinkins' Safe Streets scheme and a greater police presence, led to a dramatic fall in crime rates in New York and now the Big Apple is considered one of the safest metropolises.

The streets might have been cleaned up, much to the approval of Travis Bickle, but that has not stopped filmmakers over the years crafting iconic movies about gang culture. From the birth of the city to the not-so-distant future, there will always be a place on the big screen for those troublemakers who would love to *"come out to play-ay"*.

West Side Story (1961)

This Oscar-winning musical take on Romeo & Juliet features two of the most famous gangs ever to grace the silver screen – The Sharks and The Jets.

The Warriors (1981)

Walter Hill's film features hundreds of gangs from all over the five boroughs but focuses on one gang in particular and their journey through the savage streets all the way back to their home turf of Coney Island.

Gangs Of New York (2002)

In Martin Scorsese's movie, warring gangs The Natives and the Irish-Catholics The Dead Rabbits fight for control over an area of Lower Manhattan called "The Five Points". The points refer to the intersection of Worth Street, Chatham Square, Saint James Place, Mort Street and Park Row which is now part of the Chinatown area of Lower Manhattan.

Ext. New York City

Planes, Trains And Automobiles

With nearly 100 locations outlined in this book and Manhattan Island alone spanning 22.7 square miles, it can be advantageous to work out the best and quickest ways to move around the city (East or West = walking. Up or Down = taxi or subway).

Air

When planning your trip, make sure that your passport is valid for at least six months after your date of travel. You will also need to complete a ESTA Visa Waiver form online at least two weeks before you fly. This will ensure you are allowed access to the United States and will speed up the process at Customs and Immigration.

Most international flights to New York will arrive at John F. Kennedy International Airport (JFK), located in the Queens borough of the city.

To get into the city, the easiest way is to get a taxi from outside the terminal. It will normally take 50-60 minutes and costs a flat fare of $52 + tolls and tip. Same for your return journey but remember to leave plenty of time when travelling back across Manhattan as traffic can be a nightmare and you should arrive at the airport two hours before your departure time to complete bag drop and security.

Subway

Running 24/7, the Metro Transit Authority subway system runs the entire length of Manhattan Island and across to the other boroughs.

You can buy a single fare Metrocard for $2.50 which allows you to travel anywhere in the city within the subway system (and can be transferred to a bus within 2 hours). If you are staying for a few days you can buy an unlimited 7 or 30 day pass.

The trains run up and down Manhattan (not across) and there can be different entrances for Uptown and Downtown trains.

Also worth being aware, unlike the London Underground, there are no signs telling you when the next train is due... but they are pretty frequent and a lot cooler than their London equivalents!

Taxi

When hailing a cab, just look for one with its light on. It's the law that they must stop and take you to your destination anywhere within the 5 boroughs or JFK airport.

When taking a taxi, give the driver your destination in terms of cross-streets i.e. 57th & Lexington, 14th & 2nd, etc.

The fares are very reasonable compared to the UK, with small surcharges for mid-week evening and nighttime fares.

Unlike UK cabbies, don't expect much chit-chat as they keep themselves to themselves and their bluetooth headsets. Make sure to buckle up as the driving will seem like something out of a *Fast And Furious* movie.

Ext. New York City

Walk

Ultimately though, the best way to see the city is to put on your comfiest pair of trainers and hit the streets. That way you can experience all the sights, sounds and smells that New York City has to offer.

If anyone, or anything, gets in your way, just do your best Dustin Hoffman in *Midnight Cowboy* impression and yell *"I'M WALKING HERE!"*.

Tour Bus

One thing you will find walking around the major tourist areas of the city are many different people offering you bus tours of Manhattan. Many of them are jump-on, jump-off type deals and can be one way to see the sights at your own pace but if you are looking for a movie-themed tour then visit www.OnLocationTours.com. They offer a range of bus and walking tours including Classic locations, NYC Movie and TV sites, Central Park. The tour guides are friendly and knowledgable and it can be a great way to see the famous locations.

Dallas King

Hotels

The Big Apple might be the "city that never sleeps" but even the most hardened film fan will need a place to rest their head while exploring all these cinematic locations and what better place to stay than in a hotel that has featured in some of Hollywood's greatest films?

There are over 450 hotels in Manhattan but there are a few that have consistently appeared on screen over the years. These are highlighted below but whether you are planning on staying in a five star hotel or a Holiday Inn, it is important to book well in advance as occupancy rates are extremely high between tourists and business customers. The average hotel room will cost in excess of $300 a night and it is worth remembering that you will often be paying for location rather than space as New York hotel rooms are notoriously on the small size. However that shouldn't matter too much because if you are visiting New York City you should not be spending too much time in your hotel!

The Plaza Hotel

Ext. New York City

The Plaza Hotel
768 Fifth Avenue, NY 10019. +1 212-759-3000. www.fairmont.com/the-plaza-new-york. Metro Station: 5 Av-59 St.

Arguably the most famous and recognisable hotel in Manhattan, The Plaza is situated on the corner of Fifth Avenue and Central Park. Built in 1907, it became a symbol of opulence and decadence in the Big Apple during the Roaring Twenties, as shown in Baz Luhrmann's 2013 adaptation of *The Great Gatsby*. Famous film guests have included *Arthur*, *Crocodile Dundee*, Stillwater and the pop journalists in *Almost Famous*. Kevin McAllister uses his parents' credit card to check into the hotel (and run up a huge room service tab) in *Home Alone 2: Lost In New York*. The hotel's famous Oak Room bar featured in *North By Northwest* where Cary Grant's Roger Thornhill is the victim of a case of mistaken identity.

The Roosevelt Hotel
45 East 45th Street and Madison Avenue. NY 10017. +1 212-661-9600. www.theroosevelthotel.com. Metro Station: Grand Central–42 St.

The exterior of the hotel has posed as The Dolphin Hotel in *1408* and featured extensively as the eponymous ledge in *Man On A Ledge* while the interior conference room played host to Gordon Gecko's infamous "Greed Is Good" speech in *Wall Street*.

The Waldorf Astoria
301 Park Avenue. NY 10022. +1 212-355-3000. www.waldorfastoria3.hilton.com. Metro Station: 51 St.

Apparently the first hotel to offer room service and originator of the Waldorf Salad, the clue is in the name.

Al Pacino took Gabrielle Anwar for a memorable spin round the dance floor of the Vanderbilt Room in *Scent Of A Woman* and the hotel plays a key role in the "will they/won't they" romance *Serendipity*. It also features in *The Adjustment Bureau* where Matt Damon and Emily Blunt enjoy a fateful flirtation in a bathroom (or is that restroom?) and it is the hotel where Jennifer Lopez is a *Maid In Manhattan*.

The St. Regis Hotel
2 E 55th Street. NY 10022. +1 212-753-4500. www.stregisnewyork.com. Metro Station: 5 Av/53 St.

The St. Regis is considered one of the most luxurious hotels in the world, and being located on 55th Street, it is in keeping with its high-end Fifth Avenue surroundings.

Always a popular location for celebrity spotting, Marilyn Monroe rented a $1000 a night suite here and John Lennon wrote War Is Over in one of the rooms.

The world famous Old King Cole Bar is rumoured to have invented the Bloody Mary and features in *The First Wives Club* and *The Devil Wears Prada*.

On film the hotel has played host to guests ranging from Michael Corleone in *The Godfather*, *Miss Congeniality* and *Hannah And Her Sisters*.

Ext. New York City

The Hotel Chelsea
222 W 23rd Street, NY10011. +1 646-918-8770. www.hotelchelsea.com
Metro Station: 23 St.

Designated a New York landmark in 1966 it is the most notorious hotel in this list, although one that is sadly unavailable for bookings as it has been closed for renovations since 2011.

Perhaps best known for being the site of the death of Nancy Spungen (of Sid And Nancy fame) in 1978, it has hosted a wide variety of literary, musical and cinematic legends across the years.

In the sixties Arthur C. Clarke wrote *2001 A Space Odyssey* here; beat writers Kerouac, Ginsberg and Burroughs all stayed here; Dylan Thomas died of a heart attack; Warhol and the Factory set called it home; the list goes on and on.

In cinematic terms it appeared on the big screen in Andy Warhol's *Chelsea Girls*, *9½ Weeks*, *Sid And Nancy* and was used for the interior of Jean Reno and Natalie Portman's apartment block in *Leon*.

Restaurants

Trekking across the five boroughs in search of famous locations can work up your appetite. While there is no shortage of hot dog and pretzel stands on every corner of Manhattan, the ideal snack for sustenance is a slice of Ray's Pizza (remembering to use the New York fold technique). There are many branches around the city but despite them all claiming to be the "original", like Santa Claus tells Buddy in *Elf* the original is on 11th. Well that should say "was" as it is no longer there sadly.

If however, you fancy dining like the stars, here are a few suggestions of places to grab a cinematic bite of the Big Apple. Just remember that there will be a 8.875% sales tax added to your bill and waiters/waitresses will expect a 15-20% tip based on their service.

Katz's Delicatessan
205 E Houston St, NY 10002. Open 8.00 till late. +1 212-254-2246. www.katzsdelicatessan.com. Metro Station: 2 Av.

Ext. New York City

No trip to New York is complete without a visit to the world's most famous deli and home to some of the biggest sandwiches you are ever likely to see. This is where Meg Ryan showcased her infamous fake orgasm to Billy Crystal in *When Harry Met Sally* so make sure you grab their table (it's signposted) and have what she's having! The deli also featured in *Enchanted*.

Carnegie Deli
854 Seventh Avenue. Open 6.30am till 2.00am daily. +1 212-757-2245. www.carnegiedeli.com. Metro Station: 57 St–7 Av.

If you still have room and haven't succumbed to the meat sweats after Katz's, head on up to this fine eatery which bookends Woody Allen's *Broadway Danny Rose*. At the end of the film the character is awarded the highest honour possible at the restaurant and has a sandwich named after him, a bagel with smoked salmon, cream cheese and marinara sauce. In real life the "Danny Rose" is on the menu but is filled with pastrami, corned beef and coleslaw. If you stop by the deli, pop around the corner to 200 West 54th Street to see the outside of Danny Rose's apartment building.

Inside the Deli you'll find cold cuts, cheesecakes and celebrity customer photographs adorning every inch of wall space in this New York institution.

21 Club
21 W 52nd St, NY 10019. Open 12.00pm – 2.30pm (Lunch) 5.00pm – 11.00pm (Dinner) +1 212-582-7200. www.21club.com. Metro Station: 5 Av/53 St.

Anyone who's anyone has dined at the 21 Club since it opened as a speakeasy during the Prohibition. In fact every President since Franklin D. Roosevelt has dined here (with the exception of George W. Bush). It was seen as *the* place to do business and that is also true in the movies as Gordon Gecko takes Bud Fox here in *Wall Street* and J.J. Hunsecker could often be found here writing his reviews in *Sweet Smell Of Success*.

If you are looking to follow in their footsteps, book well in advance and make sure you look smart. They have abandoned their tie policy but jackets are a must and jeans and sneakers are a strict no-no.

Serendipity 3
225 E 60th St, NY 10022. Open 11.30am till midnight (Sun-Thu)/1.00am (Fri-Sat). www.serendipity3.com. Nearest Metro Station: Lexington Av/59 St.

In *Serendipity*, partly named after the restaurant, John Cusack and Kate Beckinsale form an attraction over a Frrrozen Hot Chocolate at this place. It has become famous for its desserts which are well worth the wait.

Ext. New York City

Ellen's Stardust Diner
1650 Broadway, NY 10019. Open 7.00am till 12.00 daily. +1 212-956-5151. www.ellensstardustdiner.com. Nearest Metro Station: 50 St.

As featured in the film *New Year's Eve*, you will either love it or loathe it. Your opinion will depend on whether you are happy listening to waiting staff who dream of starring on Broadway taking time out of serving customers to serenade them over breakfast with a variety of pop classics and show tunes.

The tone of the music is always perky and upbeat so don't expect any Les Miserables but you can be guaranteed an extra helping of cheese to go with your fries!

Dallas King

Bars

It can be thirsty work all that sightseeing and let's face it, despite there being a Starbucks every 100 yards in Manhattan, there are times when coffee is simply not enough and you require something a little stronger. So make your way to one of these watering holes, pull up a bar stool and relax.

The legal drinking age is 21 so keep photographic ID on you at all times as some bars may ID you to get in, no matter how old you are. Remember when tipping the bartender that the usual is a dollar per drink.

Schiller's Liquor Bar
131 Rivington Street, NY 10002. Open 11.00am – 1.00am. +1 212-260-4555. www.schillersny.com Nearest Metro Station: Delancey St.

A cool bar in the East Village which does great sliders and cocktails plus a wine list that classifies its selections as cheap, decent or good. Plus it is now making regular appearances on the big screen in films such as *Morning Glory*, *Delivery Man* and *Begin Again*.

The Rum House
Hotel Edison, 228 W 47th St, NY 10036. Open 11.00am – 4.00am. www.therumhousenyc.com. Metro Station: 49 St.

Ext. New York City

Located in the heart of the Theatre District, this bar is where the critics go to write up their reviews and actors go to celebrate/drown their sorrows once they are published. As one might expect, they specialise in rum based cocktails. Most recently it made an appearance in *Birdman*. Thanks to the magic of the movies, it seemed like it was right next door to the St. James Theatre which is impressive given the bar is on 47th St and the theatre on 45th!

Arlene's Grocery
95 Stanton St, NY 10002. Open 6.00pm – 4.00am. www.arlenesgrocery.net
Metro Station: Delancey St.

You won't need your shopping list as there is no fruit or veg at this Grocery but you might find the odd nut. Instead Arlene's plays host to live music including The Jerk Offs in *Nick & Norah's Infinite Playlist* and James Corden's open mic night in *Begin Again*, where Mark Ruffalo hears Keira Knightley's song for the first time.

Vazac's Horseshoe Bar
108 Avenue B, NY 10009. Open 12.00pm – 4.00am. Metro Station: 1 Av.

Also known as 7B due to its location on the cross-section of 7th St and Avenue B, this bar is where Mick Dundee comes to experience " a local boozer" in *Crocodile Dundee*. And yes, the bar is indeed horseshoe shaped.

Baker Street Pub
1152 1st Avenue, NY 10065. Open 11.00am – 4.00am. www.bakerstreetnyc.com. Metro Station: Lexington Av-59 St.

Currently a Sherlock Holmes themed bar, back in the Eighties it was a TGI Friday's and was one of the locations in *Cocktail* where Bryan Brown taught Tom Cruise the tools of the trade and the rules of the game.

Ext. New York City

Shops

If you have the luggage allowance to do it, it is worth bringing an empty suitcase with you to fill up with all the clothes, gifts and tacky souvenirs that you will end up buying in the Big Apple. Whether it is checking out the designer shops of Fifth Avenue or hunting for bargains in the Greenwich and East Village boutiques, whatever you are looking for, you can find it in Manhattan. When out shopping, always keep in mind the New York sales tax of 8.885% that will be added at the till, so the price on the tag or shelf is not the final price you'll pay.

Shopping is an important part of any New Yorker's life, even becoming their life in *Confessions Of A Shopaholic*, so here is a quick rundown of the best screen shops to visit.

P.S. Fans of *The Big Lebowski* should check out Little Lebowski's on Thomson St, just south of Washington Square Park, which is a store which sells nothing but Lebowski merchandise, with the owner even serving you in his dressing gown.

F.A.O. Schwarz
767 Fifth Avenue, NY 10022. www.fao.com. Metro Station: 59 St-5 Av.

One of the most famous toy stores in the world but sadly one that is no longer open for business. In July 2015, the company decided the escalating rents on Fifth Avenue had rendered the site no longer financially viable and it closed its doors for the last time.

Sad news for everyone who had visited the toy store over the years. One that could make even the biggest person feel like a kid again, particularly if they had a go at being Tom Hanks by playing Heart and Soul on the Big Piano in an effort to recreate that magical scene from *Big*. There was also a Zoltar machine hidden on the ground floor but if you still feel like making a wish, there is one located at Luna Park in Coney Island if you can find it.

Dallas King

Tiffany's
727 Fifth Avenue, NY 10022. +1 212-755-800. 10.00am – 7.00pm. 11.00am – 5.00pm (Sat). 12.00 – 5.00 (Sun). www.tiffany.com. Metro Station: 59 St-5 Av.

Grab a coffee and a danish first thing and head over to the corner of 57th and 5th to enjoy your breakfast at Tiffany's. The jewellery might be outwith your price range but there is no harm in indulging in a spot of window shopping is there?

Ext. New York City

Bloomingdale's
1000 3rd Avenue, NY 10022. +1 212-705-2098. Open 10.00am – 8.30pm (10.00pm Thu-Sat). www.bloomingdales.com. Metro Station: Lexington Av–59 St.

Bloomingdale's is one of Manhattan's most famous department stores. It may not be as prestigious or glamourous as some of the stores on Fifth Avenue, it is arguably more popular than many of the designer flagship stores (whose merchandise they carry on their six retail floors). Many people shop at "Bloomies" just to get one of the famous carrier bags known as "The Little Brown Bag" (also available in Medium and Large).

Appearances on the big screen include *Serendipity*, *Splash* and *Manhattan*.

Macy's
151 W 34th St, NY 10001. + 1 212-695-4400. Open 9.00am – 9.30pm (10.00 – 9.30 Sat, 11.00 – 8.30 Sun). www.macys.com. Metro Station: Herald Sq–34 St.

Whether it is their incredible festive window displays or the world-famous Thanksgiving Day Parade, it would be fair to say that most of Macy's department store appearances on the big screen centre around the holidays. The most well-known of these being the original version of the Christmas classic *Miracle On 34th Street*. The 34th Street referring to Macy's address where store Santa Kris Kringle believes that he is the real Santa Claus. Filming took place in the store as well as the during the 1946 parade. The 1994 remake was not set in Macy's as they refused permission to film.

Zabar's
2245 Broadway, NY 10024. +1 212-787-2000. Open 8.00am – 7.30pm. 8.00am – 8.00pm (Sat). 9.00am – 6.00pm (Sun). www.zabars.com. Metro Station: 79 St.

A family run business that has been passed down through three generations, Zabar's is a shop that needs to be experienced. Inside is an endless maze of breads, bagels, meats, cheeses, salads and coffee, they roast the beans themselves. Having stood on the corner of 80th & Broadway for over 80 years, it is an Upper West Side institution so its no surprise to see it onscreen in *You've Got Mail* as local residents (and bookstore rivals) Tom Hanks and Meg Ryan have a small tet-a-tet in the cash only queue.

Ext. New York City

Museums

Museums can be places where history comes alive (quite literally in *Night At The Museum*) or showcases the sheer wealth of expression and creativity within the human spirit in the form of art. This is further showcased in another art form, the moving picture. On occasion the two combine to create magical movie moments.

The Metropolitan Museum Of Art
1000 5th Avenue, NY 10028. Open 10.00am - 5.30pm (9.00 on Sat/Sun). www.metmuseum.org. Metro Station: 77 St.

It is the largest art museum in the United States, occupying two million square feet of space and featuring just as many pieces of art on display.

The Met is one of the integral locations in *The Thomas Crown Affair* (1998), where rich playboy philanthropist Crown steals (and subsequently returns) a painting from the museum. However the museum refused permission to film inside the building so the lobby of the New York Public Library was used instead.

It has also featured in many other films, with the Egyptian exhibition appearing in *Maid In Manhattan* and *When Harry Met Sally*, and the exterior steps being used in *Hitch*, *A Perfect Murder* and *Everyone Says I Love You*.

American Museum Of Natural History
Central Park West & 79th St, NY 10024. Open 10.00am – 5.45pm. www.amnh.org. Metro Station: 81 St-Museum of Natural History.

The Squid And The Whale takes it name from the huge diaroma of the eponymous giant squid and sperm whale in the Hall of Ocean Life and features in the film's final scene. *On The Town* has a musical number set within the museum.

However the museum is most famous for the *Night At The Museum* movies where a night watchman played by Ben Stiller discovers that the exhibits magically come to life when the sun goes down.

Obviously given the nature of the movies, filming was done on a soundstage where they recreated the interior of the museum.

Solomon R. Guggenheim Museum
1071 5th Avenue, NY 10128. Open 10.00 – 5.45 (7.45 Sat). Closed Thursdays. www.guggenheim.org. Metro Station: 86 St.

The film *The International* features a shoot out within the museum which involved the filmmakers having to recreate a life-size replica of the museum's unique interior on a soundstage.

Ext. New York City

It has also featured in *Manhattan, Men In Black, Mr. Popper's Penguins* and *Annie (2014)*.

The Alexander Hamilton US Custom House
1 Bowling Green, NY 10004. Metro Station: Bowling Green.

Currently housing the New York branch of the National Museum of the American Indian and the National Archives of New York, this building was most famously used as a location in *Ghostbusters II* where it becomes encased in slime and a painting of Vigo the Carpathian comes to life and faces off against the team.

Dallas King

Cinemas

Any film fan worth their salt should take in at least one movie screening during their time in the Big Apple.

It might no longer be possible to enjoy *The Sorrow And The Pity* or shoot down a fellow moviegoer with the help of Marshall Mcluhan where Woody did as those cinemas sadly no longer exist. However there are still plenty of great multiplexes and moviehouses to visit in order to get the full American cinema-going experience (eating and drinking your body weight in buttered popcorn and super-sized Pepsi whilst listening to an over-excited audience who are happy to make their opinions on the movie well known to other patrons).

Although it happens less often now due to the increased profitability of the worldwide box office market, the USA can still get some film titles several weeks (or even months) in advance so make sure to check the upcoming release schedule on IMDB.com and plan accordingly.

The average ticket price in NYC (before you start factoring in 3D or IMAX supplements) is $15-$18, which is comparable with London's Leicester Square. Of course, there are deals to be had if you want to make a morning visit to the moving pictures or head out of Midtown to find some of the more quirky repertory and independent cinemas.

Landmark Sunshine Cinema
143 E Houston St, NY 10002. +1 212-33-8182. www.landmarktheatres.com. Metro Station: 2 Av.

This picturehouse has been around since 1909 and the Sunshine rises above the repertory competition thanks to its programming selections and midnight screenings of cult classics like *The Shining* and *The Room* (complete with audience participation and flying cutlery).

Ext. New York City

Landmark Sunshine Cinema

Film Forum
209 W Houston St, NY 10014. + 1 212-727-8110. www.filmforum.org. Metro Station: Houston St.

Across the other end of Houston Street lies the Film Forum. With the widest range of independent, foreign language and classic cinema it is a natural home for cineastes. If the Sunshine was the NYC equivalent of the Prince Charles Cinema, the Film Forum is the BFI Southbank.

AMC Loews Lincoln Square 13
1998 Broadway, NY 10023. +1 212-336-5020. www.amctheatres.com/movie-theatres/amc-loews-lincoln-square-13/. Metro Station: 66 St-Lincoln Center.

THE place to go in New York for the IMAX experience. Don't fall for one of those LIE-MAX screens elsewhere, Lincoln Square has the biggest screen in Manhattan at a staggering 100ft x 80 ft.

Regal Cinemas E-Walk 13
247 W 42nd St, NY 10036. +1 844-462-7342. www.regmovies.com. Metro Station: Times Square-42 St.

Sitting directly opposite the AMC Empire 25, this is one of the two big multiplexes in Times Square. Screening films well into the night, it can be completely packed all day long. Don't expect to find the small releases here, this is strictly mainstream fare but their screens are equipped with Dolby Atmos sound which is the best sound system available.

Bryant Park
West 40th St and Avenue of the Americas. +1 212-768-4242. www.bryantpark.org. Nearest Metro Station: 5 Av.

Every Monday from June through August, HBO sponsor a series of outdoor screenings in Bryant Park. The screenings are free and very popular so it is advisable to arrive early and grab a space on the lawn before the film starts once the sun goes down. This past season, films included *Ghostbusters*, *The Poseidon Adventure* and *Back To The Future*.

Ext. New York City

Maps: Upper West Side

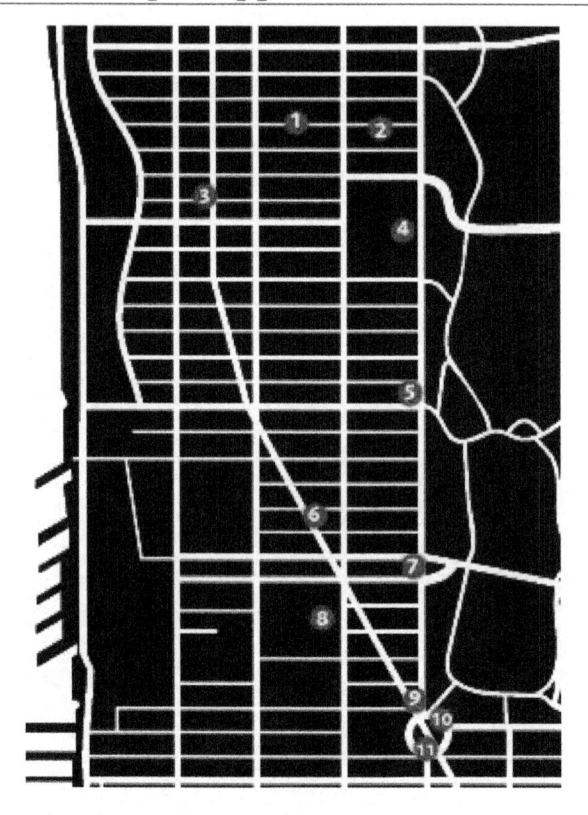

1) **Café Lalo**
   201 W 83rd St - *You've Got Mail*
2) **46 W 83rd St** – *The Naked City* – Page 4
3) **Zabar's**
   2245 Broadway – *You've Got Mail* – Page 81
4) **American Museum Of Natural History**
   Central Park West & 79th St – *Night At The Museum* – Page 83
5) **The Dakota Building**
   121 Central Park West – *Rosemary's Baby* – Page 32
6) **AMC Loews Lincoln Square 13**
   1998 Broadway – Page 86

7) **Lincoln Center For The Performing Arts**
   10 Lincoln Center Plaza – *Black Swan* – Page 33
8) **55 Central Park West** – *Ghostbusters* – Page 34
9) **Trump International Hotel & Tower Central Park**
   1 Central Park West – *Tower Heist*
10) **Columbus Circle**
    Ghostbusters
11) **Columbus Circle – 59th Street Subway Station**
    Crocodile Dundee

Cafe Lalo

Ext. New York City

Maps: Upper East Side

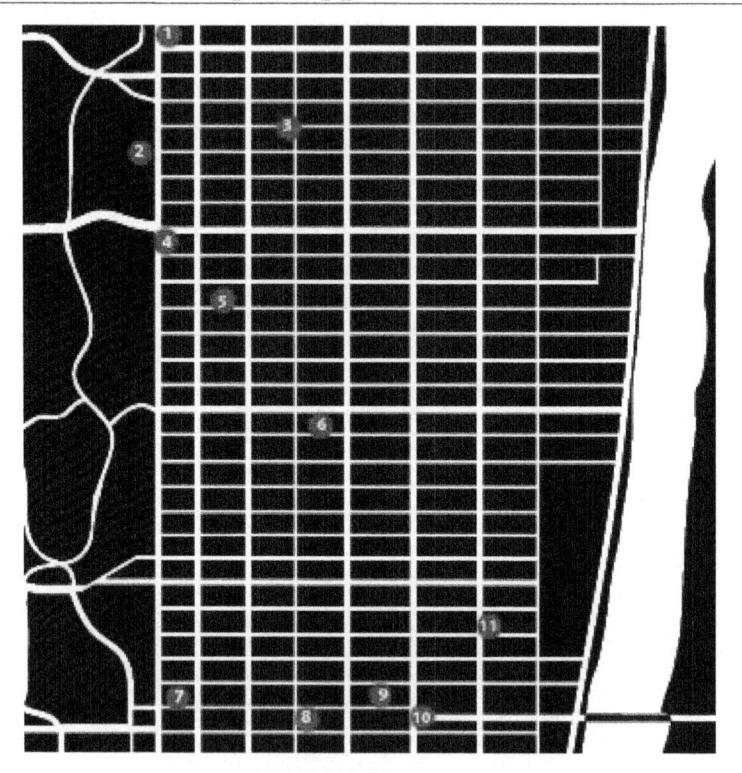

1) **The Guggenheim Museum**
   1071 5th Avenue – *The International* – Page 83
2) **The Metropolitan Museum Of Art**
   1000 5th Avenue – *Maid In Manhattan* – Page 82
3) **Lexington Candy Shop**
   1226 Lexington Avenue – *Three Days Of The Condor*
4) **The Valmont Mansion**
   907 5th Avenue – *Cruel Intentions*
5) **Café Carlyle**
   35 E 76th St – *Hannah And Her Sisters* – Page 26
6) **Holly Golightly's Apartment**
   169 E 71st St – *Breakfast At Tiffany's* - Page 16

7) **Copacabana Nightclub**
   10 E 60th St – *Goodfellas*
8) **Serendipity 3**
   225 E 60th St – *Serendipity* – Page 73
9) **Bloomingdale's**
   743 Lexington Avenue – *Serendipity* – Page 80
10) **Roosevelt Tramway**
    2nd Avenue & 60th St – *Spider-Man* – Page 60
11) **Baker Street Pub**
    1152 1st Avenue – *Cocktail* – Page 77

Lexington Candy Shop

Ext. New York City

Maps: Theatre District

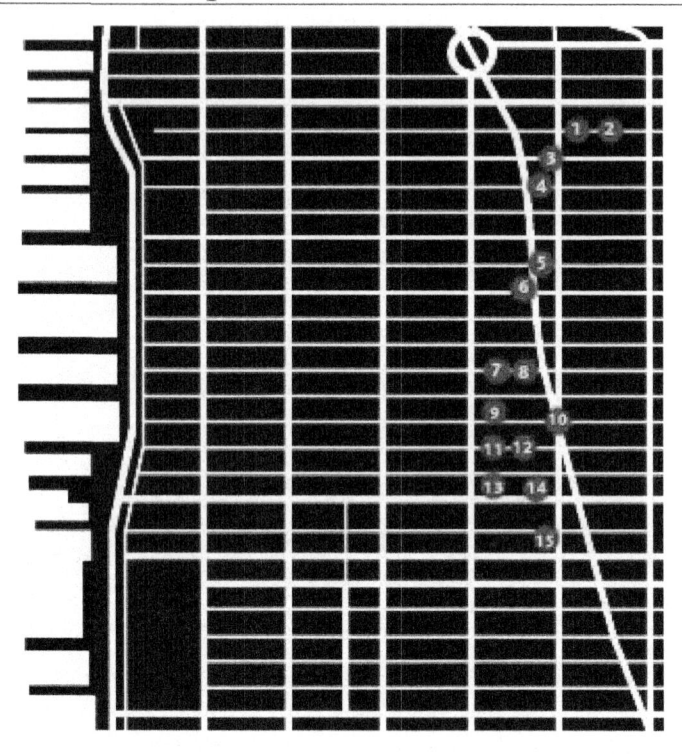

1) **Carnegie Deli**
   854 7th Avenue – *Broadway Danny Rose* – Page 72
2) **Carnegie Hall**
   881 7th Avenue - *Whiplash*
3) **Russian Tea Room**
   150 W 57th St - *Tootsie*
4) **Danny Rose's Apartment**
   200 W 54th St – *Broadway Danny Rose*
5) **Ellen's Stardust Diner**
   1650 Broadway – *New Year's Eve* – Page 74
6) **The Brill Building**
   1619 Broadway – *Sweet Smell Of Success* – Page 10

7) **Hotel Edison**
   228 W 47th St – *The Godfather*
8) **The Rum House**
   228 W 47th St – *Birdman* – Page 76
9) **John Golden Theater**
   252 W 45th St – *All About Eve* – Page 14
10) **St. James Theater**
    246 W 44th St – *Birdman* – Page 14
11) **Sardi's Restaurant**
    234 W 44th St – *The Muppets Take Manhattan* – Page 14
12) **Lyric Theater**
    214 W 43rd St – *Taxi Driver* – Page 23
13) **Times Square**
    Vanilla Sky – Page 11
14) **Midtown Comics**
    200 W 40th St

Hotel Edison

Ext. New York City

Maps: Midtown

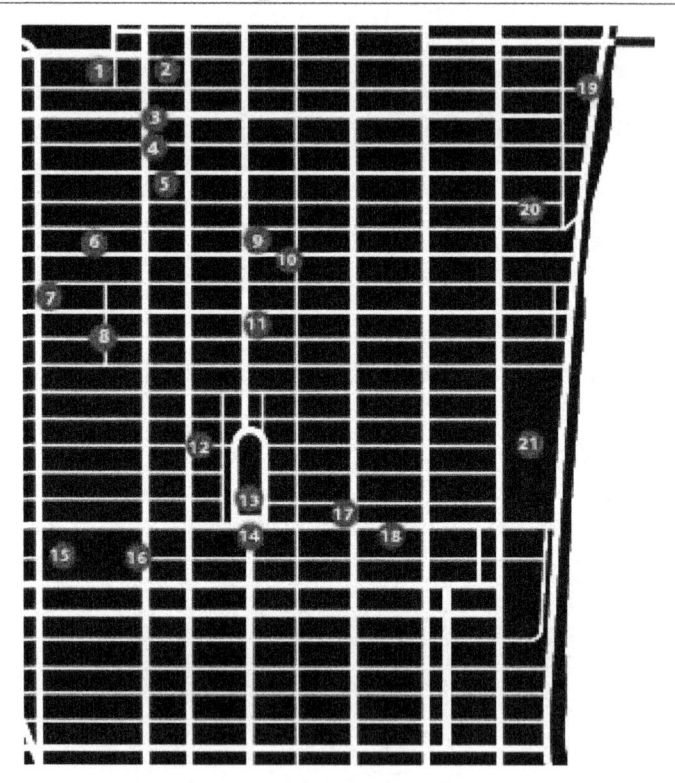

1) **The Plaza Hotel**
   768 5th Avenue – *Home Alone 2: Lost In New York* – Page 67
2) **F.A.O. Schwarz**
   767 5th Avenue – *Big* – Page 78
3) **Tiffany's**
   731 5th Avenue – *Breakfast At Tiffany's* – Page 79
4) **Trump Tower**
   721 5th Avenue – *The Other Guys*
5) **The St. Regis Hotel**
   2 E 55th St – *The Devil Wears Prada* – Page 69
6) **21 Club**
   21 W 52nd St – *Wall Street* – Page 73

7) **Radio City Music Hall**
   1260 Avenue Of The Americas – *Radio Days* – Page 43
8) **Rockefeller Center**
   30 Rockefeller Plaza – *The Adjustment Bureau* – Page 42
9) **Seagram Building**
   375 Park Avenue – *Scrooged*
10) **Subway Grill**
    Lexington Avenue & 52nd St – *The Seven Year Itch*
11) **Waldorf Astoria**
    301 Park Avenue – *Coming To America* – Page 68
12) **The Roosevelt Hotel**
    45 E 45th St – *Man On A Ledge* – Page 68
13) **Bryant Park**
    1060 Avenue Of The Americas
14) **New York Public Library**
    476 5th Avenue – *Ghostbusters* – Page 36
15) **Grand Central Terminal**
    42nd St – *The Fisher King* – Page 24
16) **Pershing Square**
    90 E 42nd St – *The Avengers* – Page 58
17) **Chrysler Building**
    405 Lexington Avenue – *The Avengers*
18) **The Daily Planet News Building**
    Daily News Building, 220 E 42nd St – *Superman* – Page 58
19) **Sutton Place**
    Riverview Terrace – *Manhattan* – Page 29
20) **St. James's Tower**
    415 E 54th St – *Wall Street* – Page 41
21) **United Nations Building**
    1st Avenue & 46th St – *In The Loop*

Ext. New York City

Maps: Chelsea, Flatiron, Gramercy Park

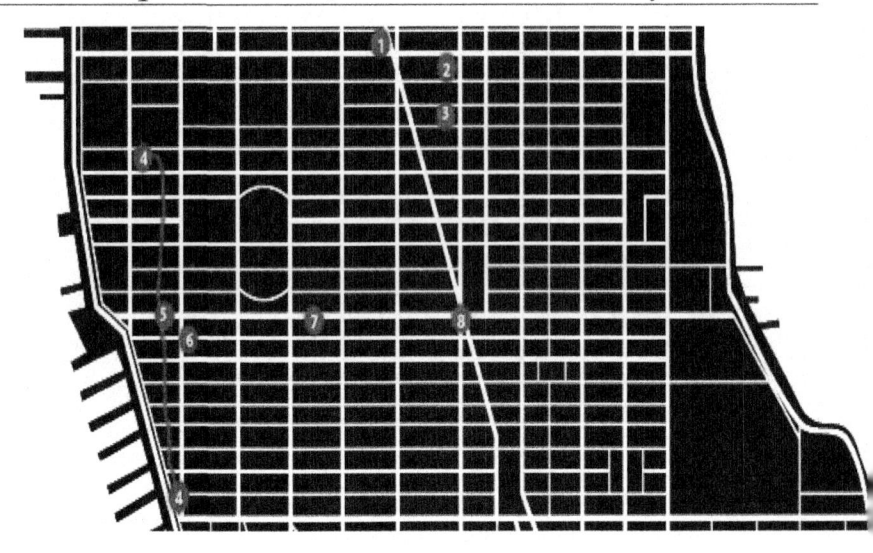

1) **The Empire State Building**
   350 5th Avenue – *King Kong* – Page 5
2) **Macy's Department Store**
   441 7th Avenue – *Miracle On 34th Street* – Page 80
3) **Brandon's Apartment Building**
   9 W 31st St – *Shame* – Page 46
4) **Flatiron Building**
   175 5th Avenue – *Spider-Man* – Page 60
5) **Hotel Chelsea**
   222 W 23rd St – Sid & Nancy – Page 70
6) **The Half King**
   505 W 23rd St – *Going The Distance*
7) **The Empire Diner**
   210 10th Avenue – *Men In Black II*
8) **The High Line**
   High Line Elevated Park – *The Amazing Spider-Man 2*

Dallas King

Macy's

The High Line

Ext. New York City

Maps: West Village, Greenwich Village, East Village

1) **Carrie Bradshaw's Apartment**
   66 Perry St – *Sex And The City* – Page 45
2) **Washington Square Park**
   When Harry Met Sally – Page 49
3) **Robert Neville's Townhouse**
   11 Washington Square North – *I Am Legend* – Page 50
4) **Caffe Reggio**
   119 MacDougal St – *Inside Llewyn Davis*
5) **Film Forum**
   209 W Houston St – Page 86
6) **Sport's Brothel Apartment**
   204 & 226 E 13th St – *Taxi Driver* – Page 24
7) **St. Mark's Comics**
   11 St. Mark's Place – Page 57
8) **Vazac's Horseshoe Bar**
   108 Avenue B – *Crocodile Dundee* – Page 77
9) **Landmark Sunshine Cinema**
   143 E Houston St – Page 85
10) **Katz's Delicatessen**
    205 W Houston St – *When Harry Met Sally* – Page 71

11) **Arlene's Grocery**
    95 Stanton St – *Nick & Norah's Infinite Playlist* – Page 76
12) **Schiller's Liquor Bar**
    131 Rivington St – *Begin Again* – Page 75
13) **Williamsburg Bridge**
    The Naked City – Page 4

Caffe Reggio

Ext. New York City

Maps: Financial District, Downtown, Brooklyn

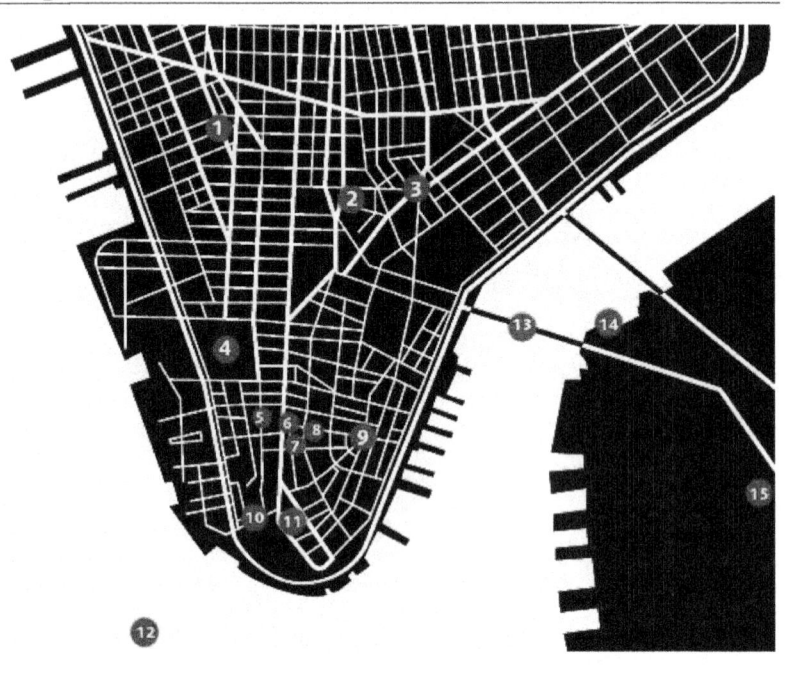

1) **Ghostbusters HQ**
   14 North Moore St – *Ghostbusters* – Page 34
2) **The Five Points**
   Worth St & Chatham Sq – *Gangs Of New York* – Page 63
3) **Supreme Court House**
   60 Centre St – *Wall Street* – Page 41
4) **World Trade Center/Ground Zero**
   Vesey St – *25th Hour*
5) **Trinity Church**
   74 Trinity Place – *National Treasure*
6) **Wall Street**
   The Wolf Of Wall Street
7) **New York Stock Exchange**
   11 Wall St – *Trading Places*
8) **55 Exchange Place**
   The Dark Knight Rises

9) **The Continental Hotel**
   1 Wall St – *John Wick*
10) **US Customs House**
    1 Bowling Green – *Ghostbusters II* – Page 84
11) **Brooklyn-Battery Tunnel Ventilator Building**
    504 Battery Drive – *Men In Black*
12) **Statue Of Liberty**
    Liberty Island – *Saboteur* – Page 17
13) **Brooklyn Bridge**
    Cloverfield – Page 54
14) **Washington Street**
    Once Upon A Time In America
15) **Coney Island**
    The Warriors – Page 61

Brooklyn/Battery Tunnel - Men In Black HQ

Ext. New York City

Map: Central Park

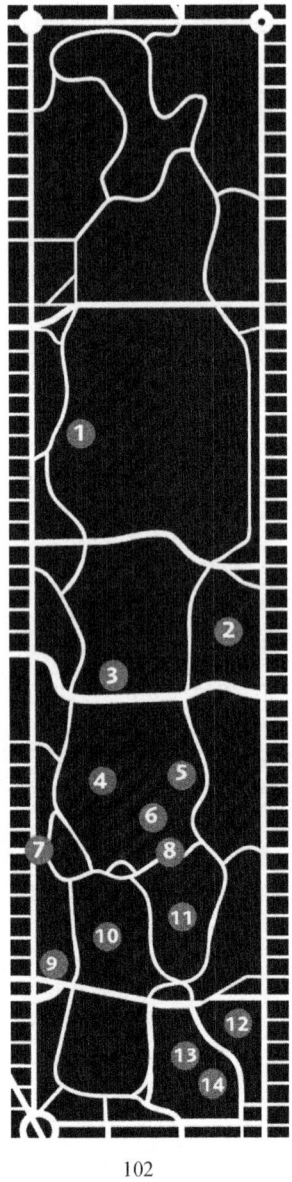

Dallas King

1) **Jacqueline Onassis Kennedy Reservoir** – *Marathon Man*
2) **Metropolitan Museum Of Art** – *When Harry Met Sally*
3) **Belvedere Castle** – *2 Days In New York*
4) **Bow Bridge** – *Enchanted*
5) **The Loeb Boathouse** – *When Harry Met Sally*
6) **Bethesda Fountain** – *The Producers*
7) **Strawberry Fields & Imagine Memorial**
8) **Bethesda Terrace** – *The Avengers*
9) **Tavern On The Green** – *Ghostbusters*
10) **Sheep Meadow** – *Wall Street*
11) **The Mall** – *Kramer Vs Kramer*
12) **Central Park Zoo** – *Madagascar*
13) **Wollman Ice Rink** – *Serendipity*
14) **Gapstow Bridge** – *Home Alone 2*

Bethesda Fountain

Belvedere Castle

Ext. New York City

Location Index

American Museum Of Natural History	83, 88
AMC Loews 13 Lincoln Square Cinema	86, 88
Arlene's Grocery	76, 99
Baker Street Pub	77, 91
Bloomingdale's	80, 91
Brill Building, The	10, 92
Brooklyn Battery Tunnel Ventilation Shaft	100
Brooklyn Bridge	54, 100
Bryant Park	87, 93
Café Carlyle	26, 90
Café Lalo	88
Caffe Reggio	98
Carnegie Deli	73, 92
Carnegie Hall	92
Central Park	30
Central Park West, 55	35, 89
Chrysler Building	95
Columbus Circle	23, 89
Columbus Circle-59 St Subway Station	89
Coney Island	61, 100
Continental Hotel (John Wick)	100
Dakota Building, The	32, 88
E 13th St, 204 & 226	23, 98
E 60th St, 10	20, 91
E 71st St, 169	16, 90
Ellen's Stardust Diner	74, 92
Empire Diner	96
Empire State Building, The	5, 96
Exchange Place, 55	100
F.A.O. Schwarz	78, 94
Film Forum	86, 98
Five Points	63, 100
Flatiron Building	59, 96
Grand Central Terminal	24, 58, 95
Guggenheim Museum	83, 90
Half King, The	96
High Line	96
Hook & Ladder Firehouse	34, 100

Ext. New York City

Hotel Chelsea	46, **70**, 96
Hotel Edison	93
I Am Legend Townhouse	50, 98
Javits Convention Center	57
John Golden Theater	14, 93
Katz's Delicatessen	48, **71**, 98
Landmark Sunshine Cinema	**85**, 98
Lexington Candy Shop	90
Lincoln Center	33, 89
Lyric Theater	23, 93
Macy's	**80**, 96
Metropolitan Museum Of Art	**82**, 90
Midtown Comics	37, 93
Museum of Modern Art	29
New York Public Library	16, 35, 36, 60, 95
New York Stock Exchange	100
News Building	58, 95
Perry Street, 66	45, 98
Pershing Square	58, 95
Plaza Hotel	**68**, 94
Puck Building, The	48
Queensboro Bridge	58
Radio City Music Hall	**43**, 95
Regal Cinema E-Walk 13	87
Rivington Street	4
Rockefeller Center	**42**, 95
Roosevelt Hotel	**68**, 95
Roosevelt Tramway	60, 91
Rum House, The	**75**, 93
Russian Tea Room	92
St. James Theater	14, 93
St. James's Tower	40, 95
St. Mark's Comics	37, 98
St. Regis Hotel	**69**, 94
Sardi's Restaurant	14, 93
Schiller's Liquor Bar	**75**, 99
Seagram Building	95
Serendipity 3	**73**, 91
Statue Of Liberty, The	**17**, 100
Subway Grill	95
Sutton Place	29, 95

Tiffany's	16, **79**, 94
Times Square	10, **11**, 93
Trinity Church	100
Trump International Tower and Hotel	89
Trump Tower	94
21 Club	10, 40, **73**, 94
United Nations Building	95
United States Custom House	84, 100
United States Supreme Court House	40, 100
Vazac's Horseshoe Bar	77, 98
Valmont Mansion	90
Waldorf Astoria	**68**, 95
Wall Street	40, 100
Washington Square Park	48, **49**, 98
Washington Street	100
W 31st St, 9	46, 96
W 54th St, 200	92
W 83rd St, 46	4, 88
Williamsburg Bridge	4, 99
World Trade Center/Ground Zero	52, 100

Ext. New York City

Filmography

Across 110*th* Street
Adjustment Bureau, The
After Hours
Age Of Innocence, The
All About Eve
Almost Famous
Amazing Spider-Man 2, The
American Psycho
An Affair To Remember
Annie (2014)
Annie Hall
Armageddon
Arthur
Avengers, The (2012)
Back To The Future
Basket Case
Batman And Robin
Batman Vs Superman
Begin Again
Big
Big Lebowski, The
Birdman
Black Swan
Breakfast At Tiffany's
Broadway Danny Rose
Bullets Over Broadway
Cabaret
Captain America: The First Avenger
Chelsea Girls
C.H.U.D.
Cloverfield
Cocktail
Confessions Of A Shopaholic
Crocodile Dundee
Cruel Intentions
Cruising

Da Vinci Code, The
Dark Knight Rises, The
Day After Tomorrow, The
Deep Impact
Definitely Maybe
Delivery Man
Devil Wears Prada, The
Die Hard With A Vengeance
Dirty Dancing
Do The Right Thing
Down With Love
Dressed To Kill
Elf
Enchanted
Escape From New York
Everyone Says I Love You
Fatal Attraction
Fifty Shades Of Grey
First Wives Club, The
Fisher King, The
42*nd* Street
1408
Frankenhooker
Friday The 13*th*
French Connection, The
Friends With Benefits
Gangs Of New York
Ghostbusters
Ghostbusters II
Godfather, The
Going The Distance
Goodfellas
Great Gatsby, The
Hannah And Her Sisters
Hitch
Home Alone 2
I Am Legend

Ext. New York City

Independence Day
Inside Llewyn Davis
Inside Man
International, The
John Wick
Jungle Fever
King Of Comedy, The
King Kong (1933)
King Kong (2005)
Kramer Vs Kramer
Leon
Les Miserables
Madagascar
Maid In Manhattan
Mamma Mia
Man Of Steel
Man On A Ledge
Manhattan
Manhattan Murder Mystery
Mean Streets
Men In Black
Men In Black II
Miracle On 34*th* Street
Miss Congeniality
Mistress America
Mo Better Blues
Moonstruck
Morning Glory
Mr. Popper's Penguins
Muppets Take Manhattan, The
Naked City, The
National Treasure
New Year's Eve
New York, New York
New York Winter's Tale, A
Nick & Norah's Infinite Playlist
Night At The Museum
9 ½ Weeks
North By Northwest
Oblivion
On The Town

Once Upon A Time In America
Other Guys, The
Percy Jackson And The Lightning Thief
Perfect Murder, A
Planet Of The Apes
Poseidon Adventure, The
Producers, The (1967)
Producers, The (2005)
Radio Days
Revolutionary Road
Rosemary's Baby
Room, The
Saboteur
Scent Of A Woman
Scrooged
Serendipity
Serpico
Seven Year Itch, The
Sex And The City
Shame
Shining, The
Sid And Nancy
Sleepless In Seattle
Sorrow And The Pity, The
Spider-Man
Splash
Squid And The Whale, The
Stuart Little
Summer Of Sam
Superman
Sweet Smell Of Success
Taxi Driver
That Awkward Moment
They Came Together
Thomas Crown Affair, The
Three Days Of The Condor
Titanic
Tootsie
Tower Heist
Trading Places

Trainwreck
25th Hour
Two Days In New York
2001: A Space Odyssey
You've Got Mail
Vanilla Sky
Wall Street
War Of The Worlds (2005)

Warriors, The
West Side Story
When Harry Met Sally
Whiplash
Wolf Of Wall Street, The
Working Girl
X-Men
Zombie Flesh Eaters

Printed in Great Britain
by Amazon